CAN'T BREAK THE AFRICAN SPIRIT

Sam P Jalloh

Fisher King Publishing

CAN'T BREAK THE AFRICAN SPIRIT

Print ISBN 978-1-914560-49-1
Digital ISBN 978-1-914560-64-4

Published by
Fisher King Publishing
fisherkingpublishing.co.uk

Images of author courtesy of Patrick Trollope

A book for anyone who
cares for humanity.

To Leigh!

Wishing you all the best, and enjoy the read!

CONTENTS

DEDICATION

This book is dedicated to all Africans struggling both in Africa and around the world. For freedom, equality, and justice, and all those that are suffering under senseless brutality, civil wars, violence, racial abuse, sexual abuse and injustice within the African communities and abroad. Your ongoing struggles, pain and bloodshed will not be in vain. It is also for those strong men and women who have lost their lives fighting for freedom, justice and equality for us and our people, and for the development of Africa. It is to all the people around the world, regardless of their race, that stand in solidarity and the bond of the natural human spirit.

A special dedication goes to my wonderful mama, Mrs Hawa Jalloh, the strongest woman in the world, for her endless love and support for me and my siblings.

ACKNOWLEDGEMENTS

A special thanks to my amazing twin daughters, Sierra Hawa Jalloh and Sahara Hawa Jalloh, for their critical advice and support. I love them both to the moon and back. They are my backbone and my best supporters.

I want to thank all the amazing people who have contributed to this book and to my life for their great help and support over the years. Without them, many things in my life would have not been possible or accomplished. I love all of them and I thank them dearly from the bottom of my heart. I cannot name everyone here, but you know who you are.

A special thanks to the people on the island of Mallorca for all their love. Mallorca is one of my favourite places in the world, and where I do some of my writing.

Alex PS, Anders Borg, Andy Dowsett, Ahmed Tiamiyu, Alan Taylor, Anne Spinola, Bruce Moore, Dr Fiona Helen Moore, Ben Moore, Carolyne Wekesa, Chazz Khan, Christina Berchtold, Alex Berchtold, Birgit and Horst Berchtold, William Forrest, Catie Hardy, Cherrdor Daramy, Chris M Hardy, Cameron M Hardy, Johnathan Sheldon, Noah Bukari Bagerbaseh, Patrick Trollope, Nathan Freear, Alan Kennedy, David Armstrong, Dianne Kirby, Cameron Maerevoet, Carlos Hollyman, Dave Hillier, Sarah Hillier, Jacob Whalley, Juan Martinez,

Joe Barnes, Steve Vincent, John Case, Sylvie Guignier, Sylvia Raciti, Daniel D Hollyman, Dave Fowler, Ibrahim Okon Koroma, Marcus G L Croman, Lukas Fedrich, Bruce Poritzky, Virginie Poritzky, Elijah Poritzky, Kelfala Jalloh, Kama Jalloh, Isatu Jalloh, Momie Jalloh, Thomas and Sarah Debrah, Tom Harding-Assinder, Tony Paglia, Andile Masuku, Maryam Maruf, Richard Askam, Isaac Fenin, Robin and Bren Baynes, Romina Baldassini, Emma Neppl, Sal Bolton, Keith Jenkins, Liam Hanlon, John Marah, Tracie Jalloh, Bryan Brumant, Javier Nobre Luccini, Julie and Evie Schofield, Mike Dandy, Roy and Nina Anstensen, Philip Akibogun, Ishmail Dyfan Kamara, Amidu Dumbuya, David Young, Helena and Anthony Culshaw.

Pat Hughes, Walter Kudzanai Chitopo, Justin Sandmann, Ramzi Merchagi, Ebrima Touray, Michael Backerman, Sophie Clarke, Zina Leseanu. Edward, Sharon, Ellie and George Lattimer. Justin Finlayson, Katrin Scaroni, Danny Scaroni, Master - Dan Thomas, Miguel Delforo, Roy Basnett, Paul Dobson, and Mama Gloria.

I also want to thank BBC Outlook, BBC Northwest, BBC Radio Four Saturday Live, BBC Merseyside, LTA, PTR, USTA, Wimbledon Gallery, Wimbledon Library, Head Tennis, FBBC Rainford, BBN Radio Sierra Leone, Star TV, AYV TV, SLBC TV, Tri-4-Life, Rafiki Tennis, Gambia Tennis Association, Southport and Birkdale Hockey Club, Tennis Lancashire, Aughton Lawn Tennis Club, Sphynx Tennis Club, Rainford Tennis Club, Northern Vision, Smash Sports Marketing, The Fallibroome Academy, Wilson Tennis, Shoes to Share, Holistic realignment, VAMPHire.com, Vibrant Concept, Liverpool Heartbeat Foundation, Shabani Tennis Academy, The Hub Liverpool, United Borders, Unite Martial Arts Academy, MD Creatives, Furman University, Southport and Waterloo Athletics Club, Kairaba Upper Secondary School, The Arcade Sports Shop, and The Season Coffee – Bar – Kitchen Southport.

A big thanks to my editor Zach Greaves and the team at Artus.

My deepest gratitude to my wonderful publisher Rick Armstrong and the amazing team at Fisher King Publishing.

The list of people who have helped, motivated and inspired me is much longer than those I have mentioned here. For anyone who I have missed please be certain of my deepest thanks for your presence in my life.

FOREWORD

A Message to You, The Reader - Financial Supremacy

It is hard for certain people to accept that we are living in a world dominated by a small number of supremacists. That everything is governed by them and focussed on the profit they make and the control they hold over the population. Once you see the interwoven nature of things that each play a part in ensuring our compliance, you cannot unsee it. You can easily connect the following and clearly will be able to add to this list of things that are under the control of a very few people:

Education
Wars
Military
Munitions
Economy
Banks
Technology
Media
History
Movies
Entertainment

Sport

Natural wealth

Law

Globalisation

Religion

Human and animal health

Pharmaceuticals

And so on...

The supremacist has benefitted from everything on Earth. They are the minority yet dominate the majority with their iron fist of rule, putting fear into the soul of humanity. They own everything from everywhere and they own everyone. They treat people as property and, despite dark times in history and the amount of wisdom we should have acquired, we are more their property than ever before.

In fact, the supremacists have been changing laws around the world so quickly that it is hard to keep up. These laws enshrine them as the owners of the citizens of Earth and give them full protection to do with us as they please; we are products, they own us.

There is a distinct difference between the ordinary citizens of this Earth and the supremacists. The ordinary citizens care about others no matter what their race, religion, culture, or status. They will support and help others. The supremacist doesn't care about anything but their own agenda, their greed and thirst for superiority and control. They will kill, torture, and enslave anyone for profit without consequence. They make the guns and sell them to the innocent to kill, then they stand on a platform and give forth about peace.

They will throw bombs on a nation and kill millions of children, women, and men. They show no mercy. They will send their army to torture and kill anyone that stands in their way because only they have the right to do so. They use the very same justice that they created to subjugate and to justify their evil deeds. They make their own laws which protect their own interests. They pay lawyers to ring fence their rights yet, they travel the world preaching about freedom, justice, equality, and democracy.

This is the group that has caused poverty, created wars, built and sold guns to the poor. Whilst they kill, they will take wealth to increase their own prosperity and then point the finger at victims claiming that they are corrupt and the violent.

The supremacist's currency is the only tender which is legal to use around the world and its value designed to meet their ends only.

They have a secret service that will kill all good leaders in other nations and replace them with corrupt ones that will stay in power to feed greed. They extract resources from every rich nation. They corrupt, change laws, kill a nation's wisest and strongest, and destroy every aspect of a culture. They then turn around and call them 'Third World' countries. The supremacists do not have many natural resources, but their homes and banks are full of everything. They go to someone else's country, take their land, call it their own, but they will not let others touch their homeland.

There is no one more violent, wicked, evil, racist, hypocritical, lawless, greedy, selfish, disrespectful, unreligious, and corrupt in this world than the supremacist.

You are about to enter the dungeon of colonisation and imperialism, the torturing and murdering of millions of Africans and others for the benefit of supremacy and power. These are the unspoken truths that are omitted from today's educational curriculum, mainstream media, and public libraries - especially outside of Africa.

By the time you get to the end of this book, you will know whether you truly love humanity, or you just love your status of being superior and better than others. You have been led to believe a history written, not as it happened, but as they want you to believe it happened by an education system that is manipulated by supremacist desires to form your thinking into one of compliance.

First of all, a big thank you for choosing to read this book. It is my intention to help people understand the reality of our thousand-year struggle as Africans but also to say that the issues I raise are not confined to one continent but can be found everywhere.

If you support humanity and not supremacy, then you should share this message with your friends, family and loved ones, and spread the truth and rightful purpose of equality for all.

'Africa is not a country; it's the second largest continent on Earth with 54 nations, over 2,000 languages, more than 3,000 ethnic groups, the most diverse in culture and skin tone, more than 1.4 billion people and the richest continent on planet Earth. And to show you how big Africa is compared to the misconception on maps... USA, China, India, the whole of eastern Europe, Japan, Germany, France, UK, Spain, and Italy could all fit in Africa with space left.'

We are living in a global system of organisations, businesses, governments, and philanthropists. Together they act like an octopus. Spreading their tentacles throughout Africa, sucking the life and freedom out of its citizens while pretending to help them politically, economically, educationally, socially, and innovatively.

It is time for Africa to rise and let its people take full ownership of its lands and resources, and aspire to build better economic, health care and educational systems.

It is time to re-evaluate Africa's dependence on loans and financial aid that is serving no other purpose than to benefit those who endlessly dole them out. This dependence continues to control the continent's wealth, resources, and politics, thereby deliberately forcing Africa to remain impoverished and easy to exploit.

Corruption is always associated with the name Africa! For centuries, the Western world has, and still does control this continent. More recently, China has joined in the good company, why: because Africa is the richest place on Earth in terms of its natural resources. Subsequently, Africa suffers a very dark history. In fact, more than five hundred years of exploitation and so-called 'colonisation' has, without doubt, caused the worst crimes in the history of the human race.

For me, things have not changed much in the last fifty years since African nations became 'independent'. Africa has not developed its abundant wealth of natural resource due to internal and external corruption. While the rest of the world benefits from Africa, it will continue to hinder its potential for growth and development. They will not provide support to the African leaders that are uncorrupted, nor will they seek to advance the interest of the people of Africa.

My advice is that we as Africans must be prepared to unite and stand as one to make the changes needed and develop our continent for the advancement of its people and the world beyond. We must change our mindset, refrain from using terms like 'Anglophone' or 'Francophone'; we are neither – we are Africans.

As Bob Marley said, "Emancipate yourself from mental slavery, none but ourselves can free our minds."

Sam P Jalloh

ABOUT THE AUTHOR

After surviving my birth in Sierra Leone, a country that continues to have one of the highest neonatal and infant mortality rates in the world, I went on to be the first boy in my family to celebrate my second birthday - unlike my three brothers born before me. At the age of six, I was adopted from my biological parents to a new home where I faced constant punishment from my adopted family.

Born to parents who had eleven children, my childhood was disrupted when I was only nine years old by a civil war which engulfed my entire nation. It lasted eleven years, taking the lives of over 120,000 innocent people, including some of my own family members and friends.

By the age of thirteen, I found myself competing in a strange sport that I once thought was only played by rich white people: tennis. My dream was to win the biggest prize of qualifying for the Sierra Leone Junior National Team and to use the $250 allowance to feed my family and pay my school fees. This dream was shattered time after time.

Approaching the age of seventeen, time was running out for me to qualify for the Sierra Leone Junior (under 18) National Team. My country was taking the full hit of the bloody civil war, but I found myself in a position to grasp one more chance to turn my dream into reality.

I was more determined than ever to take that chance. Whilst bearing the loss of loved ones and close friends in a civil war that I did not understand, I battled hunger and starvation in a country where many of the younger generation were forced to become child soldiers or suffer a painful death along with so many of my countrymen and women, yet I survived.

In my first autobiography, 'How Tennis Saved My Life', I gave a mind-blowing account of my experiences during the war, my family and friends' harsh existence and how they survived what life and man threw at them. The narrative takes us on a gripping journey from birth to manhood through experiences ranging from extreme despair to heart-warming triumph. Indeed, I have resiliently zig-zagged my way through a life of countless catastrophes and some opportune blessings and lived to tell my story. My intention is to inspire while putting forward a perspective that may be a real eye-opener for those fortunate enough not to have encountered the sorts of adversities in life that I have navigated. It is often the case that we only truly value life upon having faced a close call with tragedy then boom, many of the things we took for granted become the most precious things in our lives. In my own words, I share my dogged determination to endure, to plough through pain and dangers, to fight to stay alive, to see one more sunrise, one more day, and to smile one more time at my beloved mum.

Today, I enjoy my career as an International Tennis Coach touring with players from across the planet. As a physical, nutritional, and mental coach, I plumb my own experiences of adversity and precarious survival into inspiring my students and my readers to succeed.

Across, Europe, Africa, America, Middle East and Australia, I strive to make my presentations motivational, to hearten and exhilarate people of all ages with reflections on my journey, my family and how tennis saved my life. In 2019 I spoke at the TEDx Youth Conference in Manchester, England, where I shared the events of my life from childhood, to surviving the bloody civil war in my country. With a full documentary interview with BBC World Service, I also appeared on BBC TV Northwest and the famous BBC Radio Four Saturday Live show in London in 2020, alongside famous British actress Fay Ripley, ex- 'Gladiator' star Dr Zoe Williams, and the 'Lady in the Mini', ex-racing driver Christabel Carlisle.

In November 2020, I received the prestigious BBC Outlook Inspirations Award in recognition of the publication of my inspirational story and autobiography published in April 2019 and for my appearance on the BBC World Service Radio, where I shared my struggles and the journey from my native country of Sierra Leone.

I am a sponsored coach with Head Tennis and in September 2020, I was part of the Head promotion team for their 2021 product range filmed in London at the

Olympic Park. I have played tennis with and coached many professional ATP and WTA players and ITF juniors. I continue to travel the world as a motivational speaker and touring tennis coach.

WHY I WROTE THIS BOOK

Sitting by the sea on Mallorca, one Sunday afternoon reading a book, an African brother (a term used among us Africans to describe anyone black), ran towards me breathing so heavily it was as if he had been in a ten thousand metres race! He came directly to me and sat by my side, taking cover, and using me as a shield. I asked him, why are you running? He had a bundle of African fabrics around his arms and neck. He was out of breath but he managed to explain that the police were chasing him and his brothers because they were trading illegally. I asked him, how long have you been here in Spain?

"Nine years," he replied. He was still hiding by my side, constantly looking around to check if any police were looking for him. This brother was from Senegal.

In the evenings, the Magaluf strip throngs with holidaymakers, but our African brothers and sisters stand out because all the men are simply selling drugs or watches, many of them fakes, while the women – our beautiful Nigerian sisters – are selling themselves as prostitutes. I spoke with many of the girls and men to try to understand their stories and how long they had been doing what they were doing. It always comes down to pretty much the same sad tale, that they have been trying and failing to get legal papers – often for many years. Many will express to me that they are tired and want to go back home but at the same time, they have no option because they have spent so much money to get over to Europe looking for a better life. They arrive just to meet with a reality that they were not prepared for: immigration and status issues; a lack of a home or even proper shelter; and being chased or harassed by the police and authorities.

Our governments and the African Union are not doing much to help these stranded citizens of Africa. Europe and America do not just leave their citizens to perish like that around the world.

The reality is that Africa is not just losing its natural material wealth but also its human resources, the very brains it needs to help in the cause of development. It is ironic that there are those in Europe, notably those with far-right views, who blame Africans for the ills of their own economies. Well, let us consider some facts: firstly, more than 90% of African immigrants to Europe and the US and other developed countries around the world are in the categories below.

Doctors

Nurses

Students

Athletes

Government officials

Married to a citizen of that country

Far from being a drain on their host nations, these are migrants who bring economic, sporting, artistic, cultural, musical, educational and innovative skills and abilities. Sprinters, footballers, marathon runners; doctors in hospitals; taxi, bus, and train drivers. They or their parents are from Africa and these men, women and children are making the West better while Africa is losing.

In 2001, I went for a visa at the British Embassy in Freetown, Sierra Leone. I was invited by my sponsor, who was a rich man, but the interviewer said to me, your sponsor is fine and he has great intentions to help you, but I am rejecting your visa application because you haven't got sufficient proof to show you have any reason to return to Sierra Leone. He pointed to the absence of a bank account in Freetown and said it was clear I would be seeking asylum in the UK that was the first time I had heard the word asylum! Reading between the lines, he thought I was too poor and would be a burden on the British state. Seriously, how many nineteen-year-olds have a bank account with serious money in? Seeking asylum had never crossed my mind. When people around the Western world complain about Africans coming to their countries, taking their jobs and placing burdens on the state by demanding housing and medical help, please remember that your government and your economy is making profit out of these immigrants. Of course, politicians will never tell you that, and those Africans you see on the news trying to come to your country are in the lower percentage of those that will actually make it to Europe or any Western country. Most of those who make it through will get legal documents, employment and pay taxes that continue to build your economy.

The Western authorities will not just let anyone through their borders. The grass is not always greener somewhere else, it can just appear that way from a distance. Africans wrongly believe that they must try to find opportunities elsewhere. Why, when Africa has all the potential in the world? But because our continent is so corrupt, impoverished and underdeveloped, most young people want to leave. Not forgetting that during those rough journeys, the majority of our people are faced with many unpleasant struggles. Those that do attempt to face arduous journeys, many die in the heat of the desert or the boats in the Mediterranean. There are countless reports of boats being turned back or capsizing and people drowning. Those that do make it face racism, discrimination, and living on the streets and in refugee camps. Even those who find safety, make a living and achieve asylum status can go on to spend half their lives trying to get legal papers.

We as Africans must change our mindset. We must put Africa first; we must build our own economies and infrastructures so that we will not continue to lose to the rest of the world and our people will not be running away from foreign police or dying in the seas. Our people should not be forced to leave Africa because of the harsh circumstances, poverty and lack of opportunities. They should leave because they want to travel freely, just like the Europeans, now the Chinese, and most Western citizens. If you have a European passport, you are allowed to travel freely to more than one hundred and sixty countries worldwide. But if you have an African passport, you will be lucky if you are allowed to travel outside your own country or region. Why is this? When we reset our mentality, and we can, we will move forward in the best way possible. Everything in our lives starts with the mind, how we think is who we are. If you believe you can achieve things, you are more likely to do exactly that. If you have confidence, you can make great strides to achieve your aims. If you are smart, you can be creative. If you use your mind wisely in every aspect of life, you may well become an unstoppable force of nature for good. The mind is a powerful tool - great minds have built mega cities, created amazing inventions, put people on the moon, explored the depths of the oceans, inspired the young and the young at heart. When you set your mind to believing you can, discovering the how becomes easier.

BEING BLUNT OR POLITICALLY INCORRECT

'Blunt' or 'politically incorrect' are terms that many people will call you or use to describe you when you speak your mind or point out a truth they do not want to hear nor accept because of what they have learnt or been told that makes them feel good, feel proud and perhaps feel superior to others.

Privileged people are not willing to let go or lose their privileges, so when you try to explain your struggles and speak the truth, they get sensitive and are often too easily offended. One way they try to get back at you is to label you as being blunt or politically incorrect. With that in mind, I want to clarify that I am not being blunt; I am just telling the truth of the struggles that need sharing so that we can understand each other and try to make Africa and this world a better place for humanity.

I may sound blunt to you, but if that is so, it is because I am trying to express my deep pain, but I may not have the vocabulary to help others understand. You may not have faced or experienced the sorts of abuse and adversity that I and others have been through.

Politicians, businesspeople, and companies with ties to Africa often appear friendly, even helpful, and always speak with political correctness because they have the guile or training to do so, and need to win you over for money, support, and sovereignty. Not because they care about you but because they care about their own agenda.

The truth is what we should all be standing for if we truly believe in equality and justice. Too many people have been guided into seeing those who stood for the truth or pointed out the truth to be seen as blunt and politically incorrect perhaps because of their way of expressing the truth. All I care about is humanity and those who respect, love and care for others with humility, regardless of their race, gender, nationality, religion, status, or beliefs. This is the true African spirit. We are not jealous of others; we respect them and treat them like our families. So, brace yourself because this is going to be a rough ride, but if you stay with me until the end, you may just learn some new things about me, my people and your people that were never taught in schools, colleges, or universities.

In an interview in 1965, Malcolm X spoke about being accused when you analyse the real condition of the black man.

Interviewer: *Black Muslims have sometimes, whether you have or not? And I think probably you have. Have sometimes, it seems to me, been preaching hate to meet hate.*

Malcolm X*: I don't advocate any kind of hate.*

Interviewer*: There is a lot of talk that sounds very much like it.*

***Malcolm X**: No, I think that the guilt complex of the American white man is so profound until you begin to analyse the real condition of the black man in America. Instead of the American white man eliminating the cause that created that condition, he tries to cover it up by accusing his accusers of teaching hate. Actually, they are just exposing him for being responsible for what exists.*

***Interviewer**: Well, that's something of an argument. But I have heard speeches made by some of the people of your group; I think I have heard you make speeches that seem to me that you were advocating what I would have to describe I think as violence to meet the serious injuries that have been done to your people, to which I totally agree.*

***Malcolm X**: I don't call that violence. I don't in any way encourage black people to go out and initiate acts of aggression indiscriminately against whites. But I do believe that the black man in the United States, and any human being, anywhere, is well within his right to do whatever is necessary by any means necessary to protect his life and property, especially in a country where the federal government itself has proven itself either unable or unwilling to protect the lives and property of those human beings.*

That was the world in 1965. But in too many respects that is also the world we are in today. We have groups of people that seem to have the right to do whatever they want and get away with it. They are the ones pulling the strings in the dark. When those who are affected by the strings that are being pulled stand up against injustice and violent behaviour, they are classed as advocating hate and violence, or are anti this or that. The propaganda machine of the supremacists is then unleashed. They have the power to alter perspective and they use it. They control the narrative. As the Rockefellers, the Rothschilds, Bill Gates, George Soros, the Sackler's and others have proven, if you control enough wealth and you control the mainstream media, you control the minds of the masses. Until the masses awaken to truth, coercion of the people will continue in favour of the supremacists who consider the people as nothing more than disposable property.

THE TITLE
'CAN'T BREAK THE AFRICAN SPIRIT'

Some wise advice from Mahatma Gandhi who gave this speech in South Africa. I believe, as Africans we can learn from his words to keep our culture, respect, and unity as one people so that others will not continue to exploit and disrespect us as we have experienced through the centuries.

Mahatma Gandhi: "There is no course for which I am prepared to kill. Whatever they do to us, we will attack no one, kill no one, but we will not give our fingerprints, not one of us. They will imprison us, they will fine us, they will seize our possessions, but they cannot take away our self-respect if we do not give it to them."

Someone in the audience asked, "Have you been to prison? They beat us and tortured us."

Gandhi: "I am asking you to fight, to fight against their anger, not to provoke it. We will not strike a blow. But we will receive them. And through our pain, we will make them see their injustice and it will hurt, as all fighting hurts. But we cannot lose, we cannot. They may torture my body, break my bones, even kill me... then they will have my dead body not my obedience. We are Hindu and Muslim, children of God, each one of us. Let us take a solemn oath in his name that come what may, we will not submit to this law."

To back up Gandhi's speech, we have been through hell and back at the hands of imperialists and colonisers, and even some of our own people who have been traitors yet, our true spirit remains strong. We must unite throughout the continent of Africa and around the world to get the respect and equal treatment that we deserve.

The toughest competitor in any sport is the one that gets knocked down at every turn but never quits or complains. Over time, their adversary begins to doubt their own effort and ability to win as they continually fail to strike a knockout blow. The competitor gets up again and again. Similarly, for thousands of years Africans have been hit with all kinds of blows, just like the athletes that do not complain and never quit, no matter how many heavy blows and the amount of pain we have suffered; no matter how many adversities we have faced; we kept on rising, believing and fighting. In the end, the odds will change, and we will win the fight.

We as Africans have endured so much adversity and brutality from inside and outside Africa that many people in the world just accept that it is generally okay: that Africans are somehow capable of taking these blows, that it is normal. In my opinion, it has almost become our normal to take abuse.

Our continent is constantly under siege for its natural wealth and the strength of our people. We have endured the most brutal and unjust mass killings by outsiders, more than any other race on Earth. We have endured more exploitation, corruption, war crimes and colonisation than any other continent. We have endured medical experimentation from foreign health organisations, leading to diseases and deaths. We have experienced abuse and dehumanisation at a scale far greater than any other race.

Our history has been turned upside down to make us appear less intelligent by those who claim to have saved us. For centuries we have endured humiliation; we have endured all manner of injustices and systems designed to divide, break, and conquer us. Yet you are more likely to see us smiling and striving under those treacherous conditions to fight through our pain and suffering. So, I say, you can't break the African spirit.

THIS IS OUR STORY

This book's aim is to help motivate our people in Africa, especially the younger generation whose future is in limbo. To highlight the many misconceptions of our true African history which you will not find in any modern-day education system. I also want to help people around the world to understand the depth of our struggles and reach out to those who share sincere empathy, respect and appreciation of what Africans have been through and the contributions that we have made to the world.

This book is meant to expose the real struggle faced by the vast majority of people living in Africa. It is pointing to the misleading preconceived ideas that have been presented to the rest of the world.

I want to draw attention to the evil things that have gone on in Africa for centuries and to talk about those who have been responsible for oppressing and dehumanising our people, our culture and our way of life. This is about those who are discriminating and dehumanising us through different forms of media and educational outlets and thereby brainwashing millions into believing Africa is somehow bad and that anything from outside Africa is better. The struggles to unlock our mental slavery and untangle ourselves from past colonialism is proving to be a tough battle, but it is a fight we must win if we are to rise as Africans, start the process of decolonisation and move forward.

This book is for educational purposes so that we can as human beings share and learn about various experiences from an African perspective and how the control of information has kept the truth in the dark. I believe that until the rest of the world genuinely understands that Africans have suffered at the hands of colonial ancestors and their governments, the problems that we continue to see today of racial struggle and discrimination will never end.

I strongly believe that we all must learn to embrace each other and everyone on this planet as one family. I know that we as African people have known from the beginning that everyone's life matters, and we accept that we are all one human race. That is why we welcome every other race and civilisation in our world. Once the rest of the world understands this, then we are more likely to live in peace and enjoy our time together on this Earth.

As my parents say, "if you don't want a chili pepper in your eyes, then don't wish to put it in someone else's eyes because it will hurt." If you don't want anyone to be racist against you, then don't be racist towards others. If you don't want to be hated and discriminated against, then don't do the same to somebody else. If we start to think and act like responsible citizens of this world, then our Earth will be a better place for all humanity.

This book does not seek to judge ordinary citizens. The vast majority of people in this world are sincere, loving, caring, respectful and have empathy for others. They do charity work or donate their money to good causes and do things to help others; they see that we are all in this together.

Instead, my book takes aim at corrupt governments, political leaders, institutions, companies, and economic systems. These are designed to oppress and dehumanise African people because of the colour of their skin, their knowledge, culture, music, entertainment, sports, innovation, hard labour without pay, tolerance, and most of all, for our vast wealth and natural resources. Do not be like those who are naïve and pretend that superiority, racism, oppression, discrimination, political, social, and economic injustice doesn't exist. It does. It may not affect you and your loved ones directly, but for others, this is their constant reality.

There are those who believe they are better or superior to African people. There are those who are part of a system that is designed to help degrade and continuously keep African people back and in poverty. There are those who believe that their ancestors did good things for Africa and her people when the opposite is true. Some are still in denial that over two hundred million Africans lost their lives just for people in richer countries to live a better life today. In truth, all the colonial powers did in Africa was loot, steal all our wealth and enslave our people, whilst making it look like they were doing it for our benefit.

If you believe in this modern day that Africans have a lower IQ than other races, we have amazing examples of the opposite being true. Look at these three kids: Ramarni Wilfred, Alannah George and Anala Beevers. All three of them have the highest IQs in the world, even higher than that of Stephen Hawking, Isaac Newton, Albert Einstein and others. Check out Brother Ufot Ekong, a Nigerian who achieved the highest grade in Tokai University in Japan by breaking a 50-year-old standing record with his grades in 2015 and solved a 30-year-old maths equation problem in only his first year at the university.

If you believe that Africans are violent thugs, thieves, a danger to your community and your culture, then you are part of the system and ideology that is designed to hate, oppress and discriminate other human beings for no reason. Being born in a different part of the world does not make you better, superior or entitle you to more rights than others. If you feel superior to others, then you have a problem against humanity. We Africans are humans just like you.

While there are exceptions everywhere, African people are generally polite and humble; it's in our DNA and our culture. But if you listen to the supremacist owned mainstream media narrative, most of what you hear about Africa will give you a negative perception. In spite of the forces ranged against us, great things are happening, and the good news is getting through.

THE TRUE AFRICAN SPIRIT

Africa and her people have endured: genocides, mass killings, assassinations, torture, coups, corruption, exploitation, colonisation, dehumanisation, slavery, lynching, decapitation, segregation, misinformation, violation of human rights and disrespect. Despite all this, we have received no reparation, not even an apology. Around the world we suffer all kinds of inequalities, racial discrimination, hate and injustice, yet the majority of us still stand tall. We smile, love and embrace the world.

Those who have caused us so much pain and suffering are the same people pointing fingers and saying that we are, by nature, a violent and corrupt people. The result being that the ordinary and innocent of this world believe we are of a violent disposition because of media manipulation and false narratives surrounding our history. Millions of our people were killed and are still being killed to this day, yet it has never been viewed as a global problem. Instead, it is merely being labeled an 'African problem' perpetuated by poor leadership and corruption. If a European or American person is killed, it can quickly become a catastrophe of global concern. Why? Because the international order has been designed in a way to make it look like some peoples' lives are more valuable and more important than others. Anything to the detriments of the Western world is always classed as a global issue, but if the same thing happens in Africa, no one cares because that's Africa's problem.

From **Malcolm X**'s speech about police brutality against us and injustice:

"Police are the same way, they put their clubs (batons) upside your head and then turn around and accuse you of attacking them. Every case of police brutality against a Negro follows the same pattern. They attack you, burst you all upside your mouth and then take you to court and charge you with assault. What kind of democracy is that? What kind of freedom is that? What kind of social or political system is it when a black man has no voice in court? Has nothing on his side other than what the white man chooses to give him?"

My brothers and sisters, we have to put a stop to this, and it will never be stopped until we stop it ourselves. They attacked the victim, then the criminals who attacked the victim accused the victim of attacking him. This is American justice; this is American democracy; those of you who are familiar with it know that in America democracy is hypocrisy. Now if I am wrong, put me in jail, but if you can't prove that a democracy in America is not hypocrisy, then don't put your hands on me."

We Africans are classed as dangerous people – thugs, criminals, animals and uncivilised – yet we have no history of killing millions or of colonising any nation.

Nor have we caused or started any world wars, dropped atomic bombs, or designed and manufactured machine guns that take the lives of millions of people every year. We are not the ones using chemical experimentation on your population and yet we are seen as the dangerous ones.

Africans are not responsible for causing global financial crashes, nor are we responsible for the vast amount of natural asset stripping. Yet the perception is that we are the most dangerous people on this planet. It is hypocrisy on a global scale. But how has this happened? Our stories and our histories have been manipulated and managed for us. If you go to most famous world libraries and universities, the vast majority of African books are not even written by Africans but by outsiders looking in or by those paid to write history in favour of those who control the narrative. Our stories are kept at the back of the shelf at best. How is anyone supposed to truly understand and appreciate Africa and its people if the truth is hidden away?

I wrote this book to help uplift our young men and women in Africa and around the world that are lost and confused as to which direction they should take. Many are deprived of their true history and identity. They are craving what others have, what the outside world has told them they would be better off with. A dream of a better life is presented through the media and in Hollywood films showing how great the Western world is and the opportunities that lie before them. Millions of young Africans seek this idealistic Hollywood or Western lifestyle; however, not everyone who leaves Africa will make it. Ironically, most will see the Western lifestyle for the fiction it is; the grass is not always greener.

Our children are confused and powerless because Africa is not providing them with the support, education, and direction they need - the very foundation to building a prosperous nation. Our children are neglected educationally and socially, creating an unjust social system that keeps Africans supressed. If you can undermine the opportunities for our children by failing to properly educate them, you are left with a broken nation that can easily be manipulated and exploited.

Over twenty years ago, I was one of those kids. I managed to make it out and do something for myself, but I was only one out of hundreds of millions of young people at that time that managed to fight against poverty. Many of my fellow Africans did not make it and still today nothing has changed for most young people. Their struggle has been my struggle, which is why I want to help motivate them and show them that there is a path they can take. If we do not, Africa may never rise-up to meet its incredible potential.

OUR STORY FROM AN AFRICAN PERSPECTIVE

This book will help those around the world who have open minds to read and understand the truth, pain and suffering of our people at the hands of those who claim to be our saviours, and how some governments and leaders are the sole cause of the struggles of our continent and her citizens. The truth will always hurt, especially if it forces us to think about our preconceptions in a different light, but only the truth shall set us free and unite the people of this world. We may be different in our beliefs, cultures, races, languages, and religions, but at the end of the day, we are all human beings and issues of equality, truth and freedom should concern us all.

We Africans will never grow until we accept that nobody has to pay, beg or force us to do the things that we need to do willingly for the development of our continent. If we are depending on others to help us all the time, we will never be able to break the cycle and do things for ourselves.

Our currencies are created and controlled by colonial and imperialist states. In Africa today, we will never be fully free and independent from outside economic influence and exploitation because the global financial market can manage and control everything we say and do.

I have had the opportunity to interact with people from many different nations and one of the questions I get asked all the time is, 'why is Africa so poor and corrupt?' I always smile and try to answer in the best possible way that I can. At the end of the day, we are all human beings living on this Earth. I have found that most people are genuinely concerned for Africa and feel for its impoverished citizens.

I spend a lot of my time studying African history and histories from around the world to try and find the reasons and answers to explain why Africa is struggling to reach its potential. The answer I always give to questions like this is that Africa is not any more corrupt than anywhere else; it is all about perception.

The reality is that many African nations have been deliberately misconstrued so that their political systems look more corrupt than they really are. Interestingly, the architects of this perception management are the ones who take everything for free, who make their own nations benefit form the most corruptive education, imperialism, torture, killing, looting and distribution of misinformation.

The corruption we see today in Africa is deeply rooted in colonialism from outsiders that came in search of economic wealth. To protect and justify their wrong doings, they have built up a story of Africa for the outside world to absorb. The consequence of this narrative is that Africa is still seen as a dark, backwards, and uncivilised continent that is incapable of producing advanced, prosperous democracies. People genuinely believe this – I have experienced it myself.

If I try to explain this to people, they often look at me and I am quickly categorised as anti-Western or anti-British, which is absolutely not the case. Many people believe that the colonial ancestors came to our aid and endeavoured to help develop Africa through their good will, hard work and charitable donations. This is grossly misleading, and for an African that knows the truth, it hurts. There were some that came with good intentions but the vast majority that came to Africa did so only for their own self or national interest.

This is not to say that we are free of corruption in Africa. I want you to understand that corruption is everywhere and every country experiences it to some extent. They say that everyone has their price, and that money and lack of transparency are at the center of corruption. Corruption can occur in many different ways – sometimes it is very obvious, like election rigging, and sometimes corruption can take place behind closed doors such as international companies paying vast sums to individuals who are prepared to do whatever they are asked. This is not an African problem, that is happening everywhere.

The true history of Africa has been hidden and what you read, see, or hear today is only half the truth. I have seen and observed how people around the world see Africa. I have decided to put this book together for you to understand the dark history and depth of Africa's problems and to put forward an explanation as to why some believe Africa is the most corrupt place on Earth. I do hope by the time you finish reading this book, you will have learnt something new, that through my words you may see the world in a different way.

I also want to help my fellow Africans and those of African descent to realise that we are the only people on Earth that hold the power to change Africa through economic development, infrastructure and the elimination of corruption internally and externally. We have to use every ounce of Africa's natural resources to build the continent as a world power, through an educational system and innovation in manufacturing and producing our own goods and services, utilising our natural wealth. How do we do this? Well, it can be only done through unity and one African voice. We need Africans to unite in a common purpose - a society built on equality and justice.

In its long history of toxic relationship with outsiders, no nation or continent has had any genuine interest in the development of Africa and its people. Following all the squabbling and land-grabbing going on between China, the United States and other Western countries, it makes me feel like everybody thinks they own our continent and have a right to fight over it. The Western world is worried about China's growing involvement in Africa. They continue to accuse China of corruption and of using their economic power to muscle in on African issues – again, hypocrisy on a global scale.

The West have been meddling in Africa for centuries before the Chinese arrived and they have not done a thing to help us develop. Today, the Chinese have started to take over, which is a worrying prospect for many Africans because they are repeating the same pattern of self-interest and greed as those who came before them. Nevertheless, China could be a force for good in Africa, but only if Africans make the right decisions and conduct business with China in a way that will benefit our people for the long-term. We cannot allow China to dictate and to influence us into believing that they have our best interests at heart - that simply is not true.

My question to you is, does the West really care about Africa and her people, or are they primarily concerned that China is now the dominant power in Africa and there is very little they can do about it?

Africa does not have any control on this planet. Not the Americas, Asia, Europe, Australia or anywhere else. So why does everyone think that they can make the rules for us, come to our continent and tell us how we should live and do things? The answer is simple: we have always welcomed outsiders because we treat everyone like one family, and we share with others because we think the world will be a better place by being kind.

Surprise, surprise, the whole world took advantage of this, and the mass looting began. Africa was stabbed in the back for doing good. Today, many Europeans are complaining that Africans are coming to their countries and taking over and putting constraints on their economy, but Africans were not complaining that Europe and the world has been in Africa for hundreds of years, reaping our wealth. The colonial powers convinced ordinary European citizens that they were bringing light to the people of Africa but in reality, they were stealing trillions of dollars' of resources from us and taking it back to Europe to develop their nations into what they are today. Without the exploitation of Africa's wealth, I believe that Europe and most of the nations around the globe would be third world countries.

We have never dictated nor told anyone outside Africa how they should do things. We have done a lot of business with the Western world for hundreds of years but, up to this day, there has not been any fair system that works for us. If anything, Africa seems to be going down the drain because of the injustice. That means we do not even benefit from our own resources and natural wealth. Everything is blamed on us; we are the ones called corrupt by those who corrupt on a much greater scale.

Politically, China and the West are only interested in Africa because they have been able to manipulate our leaders and take control of our natural raw materials worth trillions of dollars. These sorts of acts are causing Africa to remain impoverished and unstable, and we cannot seem to find any way out of this situation. Therefore, if we depend on others to do things for us, we will never rise-up and develop as a people. We must take a stand now and think of Africa first.

Part 1 – Africa

Africa's Young Generation

For Africa to grow to its potential and for our younger generations to be able to move on and start to build, they must first understand our history. They must understand the potential of the rich gifts of natural resources that lie beneath the soil of Africa. They must be educated on how valuable these resources are: how to extract them safely and how to use them wisely to benefit the whole of Africa and its people. We must teach our younger generations about how eagerly the entire world seeks our resources and how many will try to take them. They must understand why our continent is so blessed and rich, yet so cursed at the same time. They must understand the depth of pain and suffering that colonisation and imperialism has had and continues to inflict on us because of our potential. They must understand why many from outside want to control Africa and they must understand that it has been rare for anyone from outside to ever come to Africa intending to help develop it without taking from it and destroying it.

When our young people are educated about their own history with truth and sincerity, they will begin to stand up ready to know how to deal with outsiders and take full responsibility for the development of our land. Our youth must not forget that for hundreds of years the outside world has endeavoured to keep Africa as dark and corrupt as possible. They must consider that supremacism is not in the past. Exploiting Africa is not in the past. Controlling Africa's wealth and politics is not in the past. Assassination and coups, divisions and conflicts in Africa are ever present. Corrupting Africa is not in the past. Wanting Africa to be at war and in trouble is not in the past because it benefits those who are trying to control the world.

They must be aware that the WILL and DESIRE of the colonisers to keep Africa impoverished and backward will never be in the past until our younger generation is empowered through knowledge, wisdom, and truth. They must take control of the steering-wheel that has been deliberately pointed toward corruption and mismanagement and turn it. They must steer the future of Africa along the right path without outside interference. If our young people do not take control of Mama Africa, then we will continue to head for the cliffs of disaster. We, Africans, must unite throughout the world and take control of the future of the continent.

Now that the Western world and developed countries sense the rise of the African population, they fear us. If the youngest population in the world rises better educated and energised, it need not threaten anyone except those whose agenda is to exploit rather than support, to hinder rather than to help. Our colonisers know that if they do not act now and find ways to get ahead, they will become the third world countries of the future, they will be left behind. Has this not always been the worry of colonisers? The unity, awakening and arising of Africans will destroy the power and control of the Western world. This is why they are rapidly advancing technologically, economically and politically in order to dominate, to undermine the developing countries in Africa.

There is constant talk about how the growing population in Africa is going to surpass everywhere else, and this is also seemingly a threat to the outside world. Therefore, I believe, there is an endless effort to control the population of Africa.

***Raymond de Souza**, the Brazilian/American delegate for International Missions for Human Life International (HLI), has spoken about the Kissinger Report Policy on Africa's population control. (Henry Kissinger was an American politician born in Germany.) Speaking on a podcast, de Souza said that the Kissinger report was produced in the mid-70s when Henry Kissinger was involved with the government. He said that it explicitly states – which to this day remains the unchanged official policy of the American government, – that the purpose of the foreign policy in Africa was to reduce the population. To give aid to countries in Africa – not clean water and schooling and things like that, but contraception and abortion to shrink the population of Africa because they had great mineral resources there. And so, in the* *time of Kissinger and those involved with the Carter administration, they wanted to shrink the population and make sure the Africans did not develop and did not use the resources for themselves, because the States (USA) needed them.*

De Souza also stated that there is a concerted effort of foreign policy to control the population of Africa. Africa is a huge continent that could feed millions more people, but the policies of the West, especially from Europe, prevent this. For example, between 1990 and 2000, the United States, Canada and Europe contributed about $6 billion in contraceptives. Once again, they did not help the people with clean water and food. The interviewer adds, "...not to fight malaria, for example?" De Souza replies, "No, of course not, perish the thought! Never... let them die! That's the whole idea. So, in our work in HLI (Human Life International), we denounce this reality to make the Africans aware that they have to defend themselves against the influence of foreign powers." The interview continues:

Interviewer: "Is it just the United States or do you believe China is also playing a role in jacking for the resources of Africa?"

De Souza: "China is playing a major role because they are buying properties in Africa, for example, in Mozambique, which is a Portuguese-speaking country [...] When Portugal was in charge of Mozambique, they used to export rice. Now they are importing rice from China because they cannot produce it, the socialism has wrecked the production of rice, and the Chinese come in and buy farms, so about almost a third of Mozambique now belongs to China. I was in other countries of Africa – same reality in South Africa. The Chinese are buying properties, buying lands in Africa; they send their own workers, the Chinese workers, they don't employ people of the place, they send their own workers to populate and to live in the place."

We, as Africans, must see the tactics for what they are and try to stop them, to counter them our own way, for our own future and our own benefit, so we do not become victims to others for the next thousand years. People are aware of our strength in unity and our weakness in disunity. If we unite, they will see that this game of the past thousand years is over. The West may continue to do things its way, but that is not our business. Africa can go down a different path. Rise up, Africa, rise up.

AFRICAN MENTALITY

When we take on someone's life; their language and cultures, their religion and beliefs, their education and lifestyles, and then depend on them for respect and care, the outcome will be similar to the experiences that Black and African people face around the world today.

We have thrown away everything that God gave us - as if he made a mistake! We have adapted to others' way of life even though they have used it to torture, kill, enslave, control, and take away our wealth, but we stand here now and demand respect from them!

Until we let go of what we have adapted to that is killing and dividing us, we will never move forward as a united Africa.

We have somehow developed a state of mind that completely rejects anything African and accepts anything outside of Africa over what God has given to us. We are now so divided that those who are colonised by France happily owe their allegiance to France. This is despite knowing that France is keeping most of our people impoverished through corruption, coups, political control and the extraction of the natural wealth of these countries, with financial interest paid to France. This is the same for those who are colonised by Britain, Portugal, or Germany. We need to learn that all the European nations owe their allegiance to Europe or their nations. We as Africans must do the same and owe our allegiance to Africa.

The majority of African young people want to leave and find (what they perceive as) a better life in the very same Western world that once tortured our ancestors and used them as slaves. Despite all that we have seen happening to our people around the world in terms of racial discrimination and social and political injustice, we still want to leave Africa for what I describe as the 'no guarantee journey'.

Europeans, Americans and the citizens of most Western countries have the freedom to travel wherever they want, whatever time they choose and for however long they wish, with no hassle, with freedom and with the right to do so. Yet Africans cannot even travel freely in their own continent, let alone around the world with the same kind of freedom. For most of our people, our leaders have been traitors against us. They have failed us and continue to support their colonial masters rather than their own people. We want freedom and respect, but at the same time, we want others to do things for us. We believe whatever they believe; we worship their gods and throw ours under the bus and believe in their heaven when they cannot even treat us with respect and justice here on earth. We want their paper money while they prefer our gold and diamonds. We are running away from our homes which are much more valuable than theirs according to our natural wealth. We do not trust ourselves as much as we are willing to trust our oppressors.

Our minds are so colonised that when we Africans meet to have conversations, we fall out and disagree to please the colonisers. We bank our money and resources in their banks. We use their laws. When they say jump, we all jump. The rich people and leaders send their children to receive education outside of Africa because they perceive our education system to be substandard. We send our doctors all around the world while we struggle to access medical treatment. When they say, 'kill your brother,' we go ahead and do so; we never take the time to ask why or say no. We just do it to please others and ignore our own lives and development. We will never gain respect and justice if we do not firstly respect and develop ourselves. We need education, good governance, and comprehensive management. We need to eliminate internal and external corruption, create our own banking systems and currencies. We need to have the freedom to travel within our continent without looking at each other by the badges of our past colonisers. We are losing our people, resources, dignity, and culture. We need to change our mindset if we are to develop as a great continent.

Why? I want you to find the answer.

One weekend in 2017, some German friends invited me to go for lunch at the port of Andratx in Mallorca - one of the wealthier enclaves of the island. As we were walking along, I found a British driver's licence on the floor. I picked it up in the hope that I might find the owner, post it on or hand it in to the police. We decided to go to a bar and have a drink before the restaurants opened, in the bar there was a group of posh-looking British holidaymakers. I stood up and approached them. "Hello," I said, "Has anyone dropped…?" But before I could finish my sentence, an older guy aggressively shouted.

"Can you for fuck's sake leave us alone? We are not buying anything from you, we don't want anything from you, please just leave!" I was embarrassed and waited until he finished ranting before informing him that I was only there to ask about the lost driver's licence.

My German friends were dismayed to hear what had happened. Yes, the man had been rude to me, but it was not his attitude that bothered me as much as the thought that this and experiences like it were what my brothers went through each and every day as they tried to scrape together a few pennies to survive. This guy thought I was one of those brothers selling stuff on the street. With his own house and maybe a yacht down at the port, did he feel he was too important to be disturbed by an African? I can only guess.

Our people have watched too many movies, too much TV; they think the Western world is all gold and sunshine. Most of our people believe that as soon as they land they are standing on money and immediate wealth. Then they meet with the gloomy reality; it is not as they expected.

Those who finally get their legal papers, end up paying so much tax and living hand to mouth for so long that by the time they realise it, they are in their late forties to fifties. Time has passed by working and helping the European economy. This is the unfortunate truth. Instead of us running away from Africa, we should be trying to fix it and make it better so that our children will not go through what we have been through.

So, my African people, let us change our mindset and believe in Africa, because Africa has given us everything, more than any other continent has offered its people. We must make Africa as proud of us, as we are proud Africans in and around the world. After all, whatever is in America, Europe and Asia, we have it already one hundred times or more right here in Africa.

THE SIZE OF AFRICA

From my experience of speaking to people from around the world, it has amazed me to find out that the majority of people do not realise how big Africa is. Africa is so large that the USA, China, India, UK, France, Germany, Spain, Portugal, Netherlands, Switzerland, Belgium, Japan and the entirety of Eastern Europe all fit into this amazing continent. It is the second largest continent in the world with a land mass of 30.37 million sq km (11.6 million square miles) and a growing population of more than 1.4 billion people, with 54 nations, more than 3,000 ethnic groups and over 2000 languages. It is the most diverse continent in every sense, from religion to culture to skin tone. The length of Africa from north to south is 5,000 miles (8,000 km) and 4,600 miles (7,400 km) from east to west. Africa boasts some of the most magnificent landscapes on Earth, including the largest desert, the most savannahs, the greatest stretch of rainforest, the world's second longest river, the Nile, running 6,853 km (4,258 miles), and the world's deepest river, the Congo. There are mountains which are known to people all over the world, namely Kilimanjaro and Mount Kenya, which are mostly covered in snow. The African Savannah stretches from west to central, from east and all the way down to southern Africa.

WATER IN AFRICA

According to Wikipedia, 40% of the 783 million people in the sub-Saharan region are without access to clean drinking water. Even though Africa seems to be struggling for clean drinking water it is surrounded by lots of water – the Mediterranean Sea to the north, the Red Sea along the Sinai Peninsula to the northeast, the Suez Canal, the Indian Ocean to the east and southeast, and the Atlantic Ocean to the west; near the coast desalination is a possibility.

Some of the questions that many people have asked me frequently are about the lack of drinking water in Africa because that is what most people see on television or on social media. The simple answer is that the continent has a large supply of water but poor management and lack of infrastructure in many places. Most countries in Africa are hot and have desert areas or semi-desert lands, making it difficult to store water. Africa has enough space around the continent to store water if the infrastructure and management is there this would allow us to supply our neighbouring countries in times of shortage.

Local governments are to blame for most of the water conflicts in Africa, especially in most of the suburban areas of the continent. I grew up in Sierra Leone in West Africa, which is full of water, yet as a child we had to walk miles and miles every day to fetch water from the river or wells created by the local people.

Our government acknowledges the struggle but does nothing about it. If they provided the money to construct a reservoir for the flow of water for the people, someone in authority would likely end up misusing the money and nothing would be done about it. In this situation, poor people have no choice but to construct their own wells and fetch dirty and contaminated water from the rivers, which can be harmful to health and causes preventable waterborne diseases like cholera, Guinea worm, typhoid, dysentery and many more, when the simple solution is to purify the water for our people.

We all know what the problems are when it comes to basic necessities for our people in Africa and, to be honest, most of our leaders should be ashamed to call themselves leaders.

Africa needs help. Its people are dying from dirty and contaminated water, yet these problems can easily be fixed without the help of outside world. Yes, we need to start taking responsibility and do it ourselves. We have the technology, infrastructure, and resources, so why do we depend on the United Nations or Water Aid?

The lack of clean and safe drinking water, according to UNICEF, accounts for 500 child fatalities every day in sub-Sahara. It is because of the many deaths, especially of children, in Africa due to the lack of safe drinking water that has meant that when you travel around the world, you find nothing positive about Africa on social media and in newspapers. You mostly find charities with images of children and their families dying of thirst. The outside world has to come and help and rescue our own people while our own governments and authorities sit by, watch, take as much money as possible and do nothing.

I am not saying that helping is the problem. My point is the danger comes from continuous help that means we cannot find solutions to solve our own water problems.

I have stopped in many service stations in England, Germany, Switzerland and many other countries around the world, and every time I enter the men's toilet, I find an advert about poor water systems in Africa with images of our children and people struggling for clean water. Seeing those images as an African is always heart-breaking and I feel embarrassed because I know we can solve the water issue by ourselves.

Those images shown around the world make everyone believe that the whole of Africa needs help and that everyone lives like that. It is shameful to us but mostly it is shameful to believe we have leaders who do not care to change this image of our continent with the abundance of water available within and across it. Africa is home to some of the world's largest, deepest, longest lakes and rivers, but the supplies of water are being mismanaged and could be used better to provide fresh water for people. Africa could invest in educational programmes to train our children in how to maintain and purify our waters. Our governments could also invest in small scale water purification systems for local communities or cost-effective handheld devices that turn dirty water into fresh water.

AFRICA'S TEMPERATURE

One of the most beautiful facts about most parts of Africa is the wonderful sunshine and high temperatures that you can get throughout the continent almost any time of year. You can also find lots of snow in the mountains of southern, northern, and eastern Africa. The temperature can be as hot as 50 degrees Celsius and as low as -6 degrees.

Ethiopia has a yearly average temperature of 26 degrees, which makes it, on average, the hottest country on Earth. In most African countries, the temperature barely goes below 18 degrees Celsius. Africa is the most tropical place on Earth.

Another fun fact is that Libya holds the record for the hottest place on Earth, measuring 58 degrees Celsius (136.4 degrees Fahrenheit), so if you love the heat all year round, Africa is the place to be.

There are also snowy places in Africa which many people are not aware of. South Africa, Morocco and Lesotho are amongst the few places you can ski in Africa. So even though we have extremely hot temperatures throughout the continent, we also have cooler temperatures enough for skiing environments.

LANGUAGES IN AFRICA

Among our three thousand ethnic groups, we have over two thousand languages. I have been asked many times by people around the world; 'Sam, do you speak African?' I always asked them sarcastically, 'Which one of the two thousand languages do you mean?' The shocked look on their faces is always priceless. Every country in Africa has multiple languages, ethnicities, and cultures.

An example is my country Sierra Leone, where we have sixteen languages among seven million people; I can barely speak any of them! In my country I appear foreign because I cannot speak either of my parent's languages. For the most part we speak English Creole (Krio) amongst each other, and even that depends on which area you are from. The language and dialect vary as you travel from one village or town to the next. Overall, in Africa, there are around two thousand languages divided between 1.4 billion people.

It sounds like a difficult life to live among many tribes and languages in the same country, but in actual fact, it's fun. It has always been great to see and share the diversity of our languages and culture. The next time you meet an African, ask them which one of the two thousand languages they speak. Do not just ask if they speak African; there is no such thing as one language spoken by all Africans.

One of the things that I know we can do if we are united and organised is to push forward a one general language that we can all learn in schools, colleges, and universities. We have done it with Arabic, French, English, Spanish and Portuguese, so I believe if we chose Ebo or Swahili, we would prevail, and Africans would communicate with each other in a better fashion. Those who are willing to do business with us or who come to live in Africa will learn that language instead of us adopting foreign languages, just as some Africans have now started to speak Chinese.

Having a mutual language will give us collective understanding of each other in a united fashion that no outsider will be able to influence through corruption or division.

RELIGIONS AND DIVERSITY

One thing that strikes me about world history is that, when it comes to Africa, those who make the rules and write our history seem to only focus on the negative things rather than the real beauty of our continent and its people. One example is religious diversity. As diverse as we are as the oldest people in history there is little widespread knowledge about the religions in Africa. The only time you will hear about Africa's religious tendencies is when it comes to Christianity and Islam. I have researched the top ten oldest religions in the world, and it strikes me that none of them originated in Africa; none of Africa's religions are even mentioned in the list. Does this mean that the oldest people on Earth were not religious? Or was it part of the dehumanisation process to say Africans did not have their own faith or their own gods? There are religions (Voodooism) that are two or three thousand years old and some with less than twenty million followers worldwide, yet we have a religion that is 6000 years old with over 60 million followers and it never made the list. This kind of political and religious historical bias demonstrates Africa's place in the world and the way information is presented to us.

When it comes to human population, culture, skin tone, religions and languages, Africa is the most diverse place on Earth. Arab Africans in the north, purple dark skin from West Africa, right across to East Africa, and lighter tone skin in the southern region. Wherever you travel in Africa, you will find diversity of skin tones.

The colourful dresses and attire represent the colours of the African flags. Red symbolises the blood of our people, yellow stands for gold, green means the growth and abundance of the vegetation and the natural wealth of Mama Africa. Black symbolises the original people of God's creation. Each culture and ethnicity of people has their own dance, music, food, dress, language and religion. The religions in Africa today are Islam, Christianity, and Catholicism. There are also many traditional African religions which were practised thousands of years before the Christian and Islamic religious colonisations. If you survey the list of religious nations in the world based on how important religion is, you will find that Africa is statistically the most religious place on Earth. The continent has an average of 85% religious faithful and the highest in three countries – Ethiopia, Somalia, and Niger – which each have 100%.

The diversity of Africa's ethnic groups is equally impressive with thousands of different languages, religions, and traditional practices in every culture. It is fascinating that in each country in Africa you can find many diverse cultural practices from how they celebrate festival occasions and seasonal events to weddings, religious festivals and so on. It is a wonderful experience to witness these cultural phenomena in Africa.

Generally, the people of Africa are polite, always keep a genuine smile, and will welcome any stranger or share whatever they have with you.

RELIGIONS ARE KILLING AFRICANS

Only we Black and African people around the world can understand the dark history of those who have taken our dignity and hampered our progression. We talk about what every civilisation has done to us and how our wealth and resources have been taken. It is we who are fighting for equal rights around the world. It is we who know how the European nations have in the past and continue to this day to benefit from us. It is we who know how much we have done for the world. It is we that are suffering with so much poverty even though we have potentially the richest continent. It is we that have great culture, great history, innovation, pioneers, traditions, and languages. It is we who love and care more for others than they care for us.

It is we that will agree that the entire world has not treated us fairly. We will agree that colonisation and slavery were among the worst things to happen to us. We understand and agree that the colonisers were brutal and stole everything from us. We are fighting for freedom and justice.

We understand today that the developed world has gained vast wealth from us. We say that we love each other. We think we are united. We all want better for Africa. We agree that the colonial masters have done terrible things to us! We all will agree on everything until their colonial religions and languages are threatened! Until then, the African will stand up and kill his own brothers and sisters to defend and preserve the very same colonial masters' ideology and culture, who we agree have caused the worst crimes against us. We will fight and even kill and hate each other despite knowing the truth. This is the African mentality, no matter which part of the world we are in today, we are united against everything, so long as you do not mention those foreign imposed religions and languages.

If we do not change this African mentality and embrace our true history, culture, religions, and languages, we will never rise as great people, no matter how well we do in sport, education, innovation and so on. The rest of the world will always treat us like backward and uncivilised people because we are holding onto their beliefs, ideologies and cultures while seeking respect, equal rights, and justice from them.

Mariam Makeba talking about Sangoma (traditional healers); "I know that it's very difficult for Westerners to believe that, because when a people become colonised, the first thing they do is to strip you of your own culture and impose that of their own to be able to manipulate you much better."

I have nothing against our people practising their religious beliefs; what I am disturbed by is how Africans spend their entire lives waiting for God or Jesus or some supreme power to come and help solve our problems. As the saying goes, 'the truth is hidden in plain sight.' The truth is that every powerful nation in this world also practises their own religions, but they also put work into developing their nation's businesses, and economies. They are not waiting for a higher power to do it for them. Everywhere on the planet we settle, we carry the same dependence on prayers and miracles for our development. Despite all the prayers and time spent in religious places, we are still struggling economically, politically, and socially.

My question is this: if we have spent hundreds of years praying, fasting, singing, dancing, and waiting, and nothing seems to be happening for us, why do we continue to do the same thing that does not seem to work? Have the Gods and supreme spirits we worship forgotten about us, or are they just fed up with listening to our prayers? Maybe they do not care about us anymore?

Look at all the countries that we want to go to – it looks like their supreme spirits have answered their prayers and things are moving for them. To say the least, there are few other people in this world who pray, fast, and have faith in religions like Africans do, yet the paradox is that no other group of people suffers like we do. Perhaps we should change our mindset and rethink the way we do things because it does not look like God is coming to save us, maybe God has given us the intelligence to work it out and he is simply waiting for us to use it.

What is prevalent in Africa today is the way in which religions divide rather than unite people. Christians only want to be with Christians, Muslims with Muslims, Jews with Jews and so forth. In these religions there are factions, like in the Christian section you have Catholic, Presbyterian, Methodist and now the Evangelical groups that have flourished all over Africa. In Islam, you have the Sunni and Shia groups, and in the Jewish section you will find the Ashkenazi, Sephardic and Mizrahi, amongst others. Everywhere you go, each group seems to have problems with each other, through discrimination, disagreement, segregation, hate, fighting and killing each other as we have seen repeatedly in Nigeria, in other parts of Africa and around the world.

Now before I go any further, I just want to make it clear that I am not an atheist, and I do not look down upon others' religions. I am just pointing out things that many of the people who follow religions do not do; they do not research and do not have an open mind to understanding other cultures and their religious beliefs. Here I am pointing out how outsiders have used religion to manipulate Africa and Africans and how religion is used to control our emotions and behaviours while the very same people are looting and draining our resources in front of our own eyes.

Let us start with religious beliefs and religion: in

which a person or group of peoples' beliefs, worships and practices are centred around the teaching of religious leaders. Or as described by the BBC as 'a set of beliefs concerning the cause, nature and purpose of the universe, especially when considered as the creation of superhuman agency or agencies, usually involving devotional and ritual observances and often containing a moral code governing the conduct of human affairs.'

The Oxford English Dictionary definition of religion is an 'action or conduct indicating belief in, obedience to, and reverence for a god, gods, or similar superhuman power; the performance of religious rites or observances.' Religion is any cultural system of designated behaviours and practices sanctified places, ethics or organisations that relate humanity to the supernatural.

Religions are systems designed to practise and control the behaviour of mankind. Through organisations of churches, mosques, missionaries, and devoted volunteers spread these religions to many parts of Africa in order for us to embrace and believe in so that our wealth can easily be taken from us.

The largest religions in the world are Christianity, Catholicism, Islam, Hinduism, Buddhism and Judaism. However, there are thousands more religions across the globe. But these larger ones I want to talk about in more depth because they are the religions that are killing us as Africans and impacting on our economy and existence on this Earth.

The Origin of Religions

Christianity = Middle East

Islam = Middle East

Catholicism = Europe

Hinduism = India

Buddhism = India-China and most Asian countries

Judaism = Middle East

None of these religions come from Africa. Egypt is part of the story of the Bible and the Ten Commandments were given to Moses on Mount Sanai in Egypt, but how come the Bible was brought to us by missionaries from the US and Europe? The Bible and other religious books mention Africa but again have no origin from our continent. With over a billion people and as the second most populated continent, we do not have a religion that is recognised around the world. The story that will likely be told is that the Prophets were sent from the Middle East to come and save us because in Africa we were all sinful. Everything about Africa and Africans is evil or bad, if it is from somewhere else, it is all good; we have been taught to believe this for hundreds of years.

When you look deep into these religious practices you may discover the similarities among them, which mostly involve flesh and blood. In the Christian religion, they give you wine for the blood of Christ and bread for his flesh. In Islam, they sacrifice the lamb's blood and then the followers eat the flesh. We have people so entrenched in their simple belief system to the point where they will kill each other to defend their position. Like it or not one of the oldest religions on Earth is Voodooism. And what did the oppressors say about Voodoo? It is evil and it is against God's will. No, it is not; this is the origin of our Black people and our ancestors' religion for thousands of years in Africa before the arrival of any other religion, and God never, ever punished us. We never had all these diseases, wars, and corruption when we had no outside religion, but Africans are the first to condemn our own culture and religion because someone told us that it is wrong.

The Chinese and Indians were invaded by the Europeans, yet they kept their native religions and cultures, unlike us Africans who totally adopted the Western religions and even cultures. One of the reasons why the oppressors teach our people that the Voodoo religion is a bad practice is because when they first came to Africa, they were shocked at how great our people were with the practice of the Voodoo religion, which encouraged the use of spiritual powers to resist imperialism and oppression to protect their families and land. When you go to churches today, you see people speaking in tongues and believers collapsing on the ground fighting against spirits, or whatever the case may be. So why is Voodooism bad, when all the other religions are doing the same thing presented differently? It baffles me.

What does the Voodoo priest do? Kill an animal and sacrifice the blood to the gods and then eat the flesh, asking the supernatural for help, guidance, and protection and, in most cases, for financial benefit, just like many of the other religions do. But when people talk about Voodooism, they sometimes talk about zombies and spells! Zombies have nothing to do with Voodooism. Others will argue that Voodooism is used to cast bad spells on other people… well, have you seen Christians praying for God to help the Israelites defeat the Palestinians? Is that not a form of casting a spell?

The Chinese population is in excess of 1.4 billion; there are only 2.53% who practise Christianity, 0.4% who are Muslims, and the rest are Buddhists, Taoist, Chinese folklore and so on. In India where they are 1.2 billion people, most of them practise Hinduism, but Africa with over 1.4 billion have merely 10% of people practicing Voodooism, or any other African traditional religions for that matter: we have been told they are evil.

Why did these outside religions come to our land in the first place? If none of the Prophets or messengers were sent to Africa, does that not prove that God knows we are fine? Logically, you can only send a police force or a messenger into an area if there is trouble, otherwise, it would be pointless. Maybe God knew we did not need saving – that is why he did not send Prophets to Africa. When it comes to development, the economy, innovation, music, sport, and hard labour, Africa is never mentioned as a pioneer or a part of it. When it comes to Christianity and Islam, we are all in it together. Why? No continent wants to share their wealth with us, only their religion, culture and heaven.

I believe that most of the religions were brought to Africa when people found out how rich Africa was. The only way to divide and conquer was to change the way the people thought and behaved. As far as I am concerned, we are a generous and welcoming people.

Mentally and physically, we are strong, we are also tolerant towards others and show great respect to outsiders. We have completely neglected our own culture for the sake of others. Not only have these religions been responsible for killing many Africans, but they have also made us more vulnerable to exploitation and corruption. Vulnerability, which has been used by Islamic settlers who came to search for gold and diamonds. Then the Europeans came with Christianity to continue the trend of divide, re-educate, and conquer and now the Chinese are doing the same.

Many Africans are confused between our adopted religions and our own traditional religious practices that have been around for tens of thousands of years. Once we began to pray to the adopted religions, Africa became confused and impoverished. We are the only people on Earth that believe that our ancestors, cultures and religions came from the devil and dark evil forces, but the outsider's way of life is accepted. Their religions and cultures are perceived as pure, truthful, and received from angels and their God in heaven. How can we believe that our own culture and religions are evil? Because we have been indoctrinated to do so. Many Africans practise both; if they cannot get the answers from church or mosque, they go to the Voodoo priest (medicine man).

Religion has worked well against us, for the interests of the outsiders who came to find natural resources and goods, to the benefit of their economy. During some of these invasions, they were met with strong resistance from the indigenous communities. Due to hunger and thirst for our valuable resources and human labour, they brought their religion to conquer our people. If you can change the way people think, you can get them to look in your direction, even if that direction is leading them down the wrong path.

Ironically, we only have to look at the Bible and the Ten Commandments to see the difference between what the invaders taught and how they actually behaved.

Do not kill

Do not steal

Do not commit adultery

Do not bear false witness

Do not have any other gods before God

Love thy neighbour as thyself

Now tell me if the above list of commandments, given to us by oppressors and imperialists, reflects the treatment of Africans today and in the past?

You may know the story of Patrice Lumumba, who was the first Prime Minister of the independent Democratic Republic of the Congo in 1960. He was assassinated in 1961 by the Belgian government and their allies. Patrice stood for the freedom, equality and justice for the people of Congo. The outside world did not want a good leader like him, so they got rid of him along with many of our freedom fighters. If you know this story, then you will relate to what I am talking about. You will know that Prime Minister Lumumba is just one of many whose ideals got him killed.

It surprises me that in recent history Africans were not allowed to enter the White House, have an education, or ride in the same bus as white people. They were chained and enslaved, and treated like animals with no respect, but at the same time were told that we would all go to heaven as one being. We should love our neighbours as we love ourselves, yet the treatment doled out to us is beyond belief. Everything in the list of commandments above advocates the opposite of what has been done to us. It continues today by the very organisations who brought their religions to us.

If you cannot show me that the commandments you preach match your actions, why would I be stupid enough to believe anything else you say? The heavenly story is what we have been told for generations. If I am not respected and treated with equality and justice here, how can I believe that I will be wanted in the same heaven as those who maltreated me on earth and that we will spend everlasting life together? We are told one thing and the other religions and imperialists are told the opposite, yet we continue to believe and follow the same pattern and practice. We are waiting for a higher power to come and help us while everyone else is moving forward by developing their countries.

Today in Africa, we are divided by foreign religions, languages and cultures. We hate each other's homeland, nation and community, and are running everywhere on this planet in search for a better life. Have we not prayed, fasted, and believed enough? Well, maybe the gods that we are praying to do not listen or care about us. It seems that the more we pray, the worse Africa and our people become.

I do not have any issues with people following the faith of their choice, but I am letting Africans know that we may have to put these imported cultures back in their box and take time to reflect on who we are, where we are going, and how we are going to get there as one people. We must do what is best for us and our continent. When we accomplish what we want to achieve, we can listen to what others tell us.

Let us look at what is happening in Nigeria. Muslim extremists are killing Christians from the same villages and towns in the name of foreign religions. The good books command that 'Thou shalt not kill. Love thy neighbour as thyself.' How can we be claiming to be people of God whilst doing all kinds of evil to each other? When you read about the treatment that is given to black African women who are searching for a better life in the Middle East, then you will realise that no one has the interest of Africans at heart. We need to act for ourselves.

My elder sister spent many years in Lebanon working as a nanny. She told me how they treated her and other women, which I could hardly believe. We are always the people that treat everyone with respect but receive harsh treatment from others around the world. What do our people say when you mention that the others are treating us badly? They will try and defend those who are victimising our people by singling them out and saying, 'Oh, it is not God, it is just a few bad people!' If our Voodoo people act in a similar way, it is not the people but Voodoo that is evil.

At times, we Africans can be our own enemy. We need to change our mindset and look back to when we were doing our own thing; how peaceful and progressive we were. We gave the world civilisation, education and economy. We built pyramids and great cities. But since the invasion of supremacists, we changed our lifestyle, our mental state, our religions and cultures. We have not been able to build, develop or maintain anything since. All our roads, our skyscrapers, stadiums and airports are now built by outsiders because we have lost our wisdom as we did not always sell our culture to the highest bidder.

I am trying to let our people know that we need to take care of our business first before we consider others. This is how the whole world works and it is how countries have improved and developed their economies. It is not against any religion to ask questions when you think something is not right. This is what our imported religions have done to us, making us feel guilty about questioning things purported by those brandishing the Bible or Quran. Sadly, too many people do not take the time to read these books and will tell you that only the men of God can translate them. People want to interpret what these good books say to suit their outcome, often twisting what is said to justify their argument and the power they wish to hold over others.

I was questioning a friend about Jesus on the cross and

he said, 'Father, why hast thou forsaken me?' I asked my friend, if Jesus was the son of God as we have been told, and the holy trinity is one God, then why is he asking God the question? How can you ask your father a question if you are the father? My friend got angry and said I needed to be prayed for; however, he could not answer the question. This is the attitude we have developed in Africa (not exclusively of course). If someone tells us our blue skies are green, should we simply have faith and believe them or trust our judgement? We can clearly see that the skies are blue so why should we demonstrate blind belief?

Another example is at the beginning of Genesis where it tells us that God created Adam and Eve and they had two sons, Cain and Abel. Out of jealousy Cain killed Abel. The story goes on to say all subsequent children came from Cain as he got married. Well, that sounds amazing, but my question is, where did Cain's wife come from? Who was Cain's father - and mother-in-law? When I asked these questions to preachers, they came up with some of the most ridiculous answers or excuses ever. One pastor told me not to question the word of God, and I said, 'Well, if that is where my family ancestry came from, I want to know the truth; nothing is wrong with asking questions about your existence on this Earth!' The pastor made me feel as if I will go to Hell for thinking and questioning. I am not trying to discredit people and their religion; I am just pointing out things that others turn a blind eye to or are too naïve to see as truth.

When you go to church in Sierra Leone, especially as all the big ones are run by Nigerian pastors (or prophets as they call them), you will find that all the poor people will save their last penny, walk for miles and leave their children hungry to go to the church and give that last penny to the collection, because we are told that God or Jesus needs our help. The new bank of the Lord Jesus Christ – they will tell you they need to build a church and get all this and that, but a year later, they may or may not build the church. Behind closed doors, the prophet is living in a mansion in his hometown and his bank account is full of money. He is getting richer by the day. Now they even roll the red carpet out for them, they will arrive at church in limousines, Bentleys or even a private helicopter! Our people just turn a blind eye to this and refuse to understand that this is all business. Worst of all, they spend their days going to pray for hours and wonder why Africa is not moving forward compared to the rest of the world. They wonder why people are financially struggling in Africa while other places on the planet are moving forward.

When I talk about wealth and development in Africa to our people; many times, they will quote this verse from the bible 'What shall it profit a man to gain the whole world and loses his precious soul?'.

So basically, they are telling us that it's best to worry about our religious beliefs and not about finance, materials or wealth! But yet many African want to leave and go to Europe and America to get better life, wealth and finance.

God gave us everything because he knows we will need it someday to live on this earth, so why deprive our people with the wrong message? I lost my nephew through malaria because my sister couldn't afford $100 for his medical.

We all going to die one day. Having wealth and materials Is not a bad thing and shouldn't make you a bad person. You should use whatever you have to help others.

I can bear witness to this because I was a member at 'Deeper Live Ministry and Faith Assembly of God Church' back in Sierra Leone when I was a teenager. I know first-hand how long we used to spend in church. Another example of this sad side of how well we embrace imported religion was when Israel and Palestine had a serious clash, three Israelis were killed and over seventy Palestinians lost their lives. To my surprise on Facebook and in conversations with my people, all I could see and hear were the good Christians praying that God should help the Israelis conquer the Palestinians. Our Christian people believe that the Israelites are the only chosen people of God and they should have the right to kill the Palestinians. I was thinking to myself, Africa has thousands of problems, but we are not even talking or caring about our own. We are more concerned about what is happening thousands of miles away in the Middle East between people who could not care less about all the wars in our continent. We are now conditioned to worry and care about others through religions and care less about ourselves.

In addition, how can anyone pray for God to help the Israelis conquer the Palestinian people who only throw stones to save their lives and community? When Israel has far more sophisticated military capability than the Palestinians? I am not saying it is right to kill any human being but three lost to over seventy, what does anyone think? Moreover, what is our interest or benefit of that fight? Do people think Jesus will support the war and ask God to punish the Palestinians? Well, I do not think so. I think we should keep our business to ourselves and pay more attention to Africa and our culture, religions, and development.

The simple reason why African people believe this is because we are taught to believe that the Israelites are the chosen people of God, which means we are accepting that they are even better than us black and African people. We are fighting for equal justice and respect from around the world when we do not respect ourselves. We believe that people from Israel are chosen over us because God has his favourite people. If this is what we believe, then we will never move forward and get the respect that we deserve.

I am amazed that history has taught us that Africa gave birth to mankind, yet we are among the least respected people on this planet.

The Chinese government and the Chinese people would not accept that their DNA traces back to Africa. We are the greatest race on Earth, yet we deny our culture and people to help and accept others. We fight and kill each other because of the religions that came from somewhere else. Africa will soon become a Buddhist continent as the Chinese take over country by country while we just watch and repeat the mistakes of the past. If China, the US, India or anyone else wishes to invest in Africa, they are welcome to. What is not welcome are the deals our so-called leaders are doing behind our backs: the deals that are selling out Africa.

Whenever I ask people back home in Sierra Leone or other parts of Africa, 'How is life and work?', their reply is always the same regardless of where they come from. They will say 'God is in control' or 'Master Jesus is the answer.' This is how we think in Africa – leave everything to God. Of course, when you do that, you let yourself off the hook - you can blame God or claim it was not his will. Yet at the same time, the majority of people in the West are out working and making plans to change and improve their lives, communities and economies.

Yes, believe in your God, but use the brains that your God gave you to make sure you look after Africa first. We are people that are waiting, wanting and expecting God or Jesus to solve every issue or matter of state for us. I am telling you now, my people, you can have faith while taking action to improve the world. We can make great strides if we decide that we can. The alternative is that we shall remain slaves far into the future.

We have been waiting a thousand years for God or Jesus to help us solve our problems in Africa. Our greatest ancestors have come and gone, nothing has happened and today we are still waiting. As the saying goes, you cannot keep doing the same thing that did not work and expect a different result. That is the road to nowhere.

We have been waiting far too long even though we have seen people of other continents rise up and moved forward. We are still being patient, waiting for God and Jesus to come down and help us. I will say it again – God has given us everything we need to gain the strength to create the future we want and deserve. We can thank God for all that we have, but we must do the work and not sit in blind faith waiting for the Second Coming.

Every time I visit Ghana and travel on public transport, a young man will always pop up preaching the Bible and ask everyone for a contribution. This is what he will do for days, weeks, months and even years. Their method is based on making money, not just to preach to people.

They spread good news to make money for themselves. He could get a normal job and then go out to preach and help people as a way to help his community. He will not do that – he is not preaching for free. Instead, he will use the Bible to make money as the colonial masters have done for hundreds of years.

Since I have been travelling around the world, I have never seen anyone on public transport preaching. People will do it on the streets but not to collect money. It is mostly Jehovah Witnesses who do that. Evangelists go around preaching but only voluntarily. I hope that one day we will spend time and money empowering our children, community, and our nation rather than enriching these prophets. We can spend our precious time developing instead of letting people's books and ideologies divide us and keep us apathetic while behind our closed, praying eyes they are taking away all our wealth and resources.

We as African people should focus more on the development of our continent and people whilst treating our culture with respect and love. As long as we have extremists that go around killing and bombing others for their own beliefs, then I will never see the point of following any religion on this planet. It says in the Bible and Quran not to kill and to love thy neighbour and to share love. But today, we see what is happening in Nigeria and other parts of Africa. Some extreme people use religion to hide behind while they are killing, robbing and kidnapping. We should be wary of being duped by the person who preaches one thing to get outcomes that are far removed from the religion they have hijacked.

God did not make the bomb, nor did he make guns and knives – we did. The intention behind a gun is to kill. We have the power to believe that God does not want us to kill our own people for him because someone said we will go to heaven if we carry out their instruction. If we keep wasting our time on these issues of hate, we will all surely end up in hell. If people want to accept the imported religions, then my advice is to put African interests first and seek the development of our lives and children for the benefit of Africa.

The Final Result

Last but not least, do we want a better Africa for ourselves and future generations? Then we must change the way religion is often presented in the continent, especially Islam and Christianity which were brought to us because of exploitation. Most of the preachers have been misinterpreting quotes from the Bible for their own personal financial benefit. They preach about miracles and breakthroughs, quoting the sowing of seeds. For when you give, it shall be given unto you! We have been giving for hundreds of years and not receiving anything back, yet we keep on giving. This is why pastors are so rich, yet the congregation and people around them keep getting poorer. We are stuck with a generation of people who act as if God will reward them for their laziness; all you have to do is keep putting those pennies in the plate or even easier, give them your credit card details.

Poverty is at an all-time high because the message that MOGs (men of God) are sending is that it is possible to reap where you did not sow, which means you can get something out of nothing by just using the Bible and the name of God. Many are now asking why they should be learning the hard way by going to school, college or university if there is an easier way for them to be rich? Our attitude towards living for today does not help create wealth for us; millions of us are dying without leaving any legacy behind and are wondering why Africa is the way it is. The preachers in Africa should be teaching about the gospel of truth and prosperity and that laziness does not help with our success. Christianity continues to play a big role in the fall and impoverishment of Africa and her people.

If your religion has your interests at its core, that is fine. But spreading messages about miracles and rapid success have led to a generation of people who are desperate for an instant result. They are looking for immediate relief and effortless profits through the name of God, as we can see from how wealthy the preachers are becoming today. We should not focus our learning on tidings, blessings and offerings or miracles and wonders.

Religious leaders should stop preaching about riches acquired through higher supreme powers and miraculous beliefs. Yes, certain religions have done many good things and it should be that way, but the preachers should stop preaching to us about the fear of what the devil did or will do to us. Teaching and learning should be based on positive messages that add value to our lives and communities. Our learning should teach qualities that we and the younger generation of Africa must take on. Qualities such as hard work and dedication, commitment to our society, creativity, perseverance and responsibility. We must focus on developing our education and societies through creativity and innovation instead of waiting for the colonials or miracles and God to come and do it for us. We can do these things for ourselves through our own consciousness, and by loving and caring as true and sincere African people.

The idea of becoming a millionaire through the sowing of a religious seed does not help us build a better community. The message of such success should not be preached or inherited by anyone. The example that we should be inheriting is from those who are working hard and making smart decisions. To accomplish everything in this life, we should focus on succeeding through perseverance and determination. We should learn from the rest of the world and apply their good things while making sure we do not copy the errors of their models.

A good African mindset should be focused on teaching our people about hard and smart work. If we truly believe in our gods and know how to produce our goods and services, are capable of logical thinking and strategic planning, then we can build a system that will produce and encourage a successful African society which encompasses all communities. This can be done in many ways such as: marketing, customer analysis, evaluation, self-regulation, and the process involving the production of all goods and services for our people of Africa and beyond. This is how the world has developed and how the wealthiest nations have created their success and bettered their communities. These are the same communities that we as Africans are dying to run and seek refuge in.

Let us stop the notion that we only need religion to keep us going. This is what the rest of the world have done to get to where they are today; now we all want to run away from Africa to go and seek help and find a better way of life elsewhere. They have left us with their religious books in exchange for our natural resources, education, culture and human labour. We still have time to bring this to a halt and begin to turn the tide so that we can start the healing process of empowering and developing our people for a sustainable, united and peaceful Africa.

If miracles can cure sickness, then there should be no diseases or illnesses affecting us in Africa today, considering the time that we spend praying. If we have a proper system to help us with the production of natural medicine with all that God and nature have provided for us, then we will begin to see a successful and healthy Africa.

Wealth and developed communities do not happen by mistake or by magic but through hard work and planning, perseverance and long-term commitment. Let us not rely on miracles, promises and the will of gods; we have done this for centuries and yet we are still running backward.

Religions and prayers alone cannot help us. We can achieve positive change through youth development programs and a better education system, along with good and honest leadership, and a generation of young men and women who are ready to make Africa the heaven on Earth it should be. We do not need more prayers but comprehensive and robust strategies, both short and long term, to direct us along the path of recovery and growth. Why long and short term? It is too easy for leaders to make promises too far in the future; they will never be held accountable when they fail. They will take the money and run. Short term strategies made with benchmarking stages keep them visible and accountable; if you are going to promise what will happen in five years' time, tell us what you will do this week to help us get there!

We adapt to other people's ways of life, cultures and religions, but around us we can see how our way of life has enriched and influenced the world. We are ignoring our culture and adopting the replica of what was stolen from us before being returned. In this case, we accept it because we trust those who have denied us of our rights, equality, freedom and justice.

Practise your religion because that is your relationship between you and your supreme power. We should not mix our faith with our development because that prevents us from taking certain actions and learning to believe in ourselves and the development of our businesses, economy and the continent of Africa.

Part 2 – Colonisers

RESOURCES

Africa is the richest continent on Earth in terms of its natural resources. All 54 nations within the continent are richly blessed with many natural reserves such as gold, diamonds, cocoa beans, sugar, silver, fisheries, agriculture just to name a few. The continent produces over 30% of the world's resources, which increased by more than 5% from 2010 onwards. Although Africa is ranked number one as the richest continent by natural wealth, we also rank as some of the poorest people on Earth. If you study the list of the top richest nations, you will be hard pushed to find many African countries in the top twenty or more economic indicators, except when counting the natural resources that are flourishing in the continent.

An example is the list of the top ten nations with the highest gold reserves in the world. Africa produces more gold than any other continent, and South Africa produces around 40% of the world's total gold production. That is more gold produced than any country on Earth. South Africa is also home to the second largest mining reserves in the world just behind Australia.

In 2019, Ghana was the largest gold producer in Africa with 142.4 tonnes (142,400 kg) and in 2017 the total gold production from Africa was 660 tonnes (660,000 kg). Both Ghana and South Africa made the top ten list of gold producing nations in the world. No African country made the top ten list of gold reserves internationally. The poverty rate in these countries is astoundingly high. Why is Africa so rich naturally but so poor economically? Part of this is due to the illegal trafficking, mispricing and corruption between political individuals and foreign elites, which has kept the general population and the continent's economy in turmoil.

Africa is famous for its wildlife and the Sahara Desert, yet also for corruption, diseases, war, and poverty. We can see it as the negative portrayal of Africa that the world's media perpetuates. Behind closed doors, these same people are benefiting from the natural resources and the African communities. In our human civilisation and education, we are fascinated by the bad news constantly being fed to us through media. No one pays much attention to the positive news about Africa, its steady economic growth, the development of a few nations and the fight for a better life for its people.

In recent years something that can be deemed positive that has come out of Africa are portrayals in movies such as 'The Lion King', 'Madagascar' and Marvel's 'Black Panther'. Often people will suggest these films to me because that is how they see Africa, through the characters in these movies.

Africa has a huge natural forest that has contributed to its economy. Timber is a big business in Central and

Western Africa as this is where some of the largest natural forests in the world can be found. We have to take into consideration that the natural habitat is being destroyed by mankind just to satisfy the needs of others. The natural forest in Sierra Leone has been destroyed by around 80% and recently we had one of the hardest and most severe manmade natural disasters in our history. In the early morning of August 14th, 2017, heavy rain hit the capital city Freetown. Mount Sugarloaf had been destroyed by deforestation and gave way to the heavy rainfall. Thousands of tons of mud destroyed everything in its path and killed more than one thousand people.

The forests play a significant role in Africa's economy, accounting for over 5% of GDP. At the same time, we are starting to see the effects of destroying the natural ecosystem for the sake of mankind's taste for timber products. All the logging and best woods from West and Central Africa are exported to Japan, China, Israel and the European Union. Valuable woods like mahogany and okoume bring in good revenue to the countries of Western and Central Africa.

Africa has plenty of fisheries too, with an annual export of around $2.5 billion. The continent is surrounded by water. It is estimated that over 3,000 fish species flourishes throughout its inland fisheries. However, some Asian and European nations have started to exploit the fishing industry around the continent. The lakes of Africa produce lots of freshwater fish too, so everywhere you turn there is something to be positive about. But with the portrayal from the Western media and their lack of informed knowledge, Africa is not represented like this. Instead, most of media coverage around the world show how poor Africa is; this is why outsiders do not understand that the continent is not just a desert or a place full of thirst and hunger. We are much more than that.

Africa is the slowest continent to develop. For hundreds of years Africa has been invaded by people from around the globe for its wealth and natural resources. Due to some of these past colonial rulers and their control and compliance systems, Africans are finding it hard to get back on their feet. Up until now, the Western world has managed Africa through laws that they created and imposed. These rules allowed them to have a disproportionate share of control on the continent in return for its natural resources, benefitting their own economy at a great cost to Africans.

EXTERNAL CORRUPTION

If there is a democracy that promotes equality and justice, there would be little chance of poverty taking hold. Wars, corruption and many diseases in existence today would be consigned to the history books meaning Earth and its citizens would enjoy peace, love and prosperity. I know that this might be a utopian aspiration, but I believe it is an important goal that we simply have to do everything we can to achieve.

We need to understand that if every nation in the world was rich and powerful then superiority would die, and the handful of superpower nations and individuals would not be where they are today. These world powers enjoy their status and will never allow the other nations to rise and catch up with them politically and economically. When Africa was said to be colonised, they set up systems and laws that would hamper the chances for African nations to stand for themselves. Neo-colonialism is the worst poison, killing the development of Mother Africa. Do not think for a second that the imperial states will allow decolonisation in Africa, because if they did, the unity of Africans will crumble the economy of their former colonial masters. There is a fear that if this happens, Africa will seek reparation from the colonial states for all the damage they have caused. The Western world will continue to supress Africa's way of governance, decisions and development whilst shaping its future to suit their aims, not those of the people of the continent.

Do you ever wonder where the idea of paper money came from and why? Every country's currency is valued by the amount of gold reserved. Paper money is basically worthless without natural wealth or the extraction of natural resources such as gold, diamonds, silver, oil, and other minerals. Africa has an abundance of this natural wealth but seemingly has not got the capability to print and create its own paper money. Why would that be? What keeps it so?

Western paper money today is maintained to be worth more than any natural resource. All the financial controls, systems and regulation are set by the Western world. Their currencies are valued to the point where everything in the world today is valued by the US dollar, British pound sterling or the European euro. Do you ever wonder why?

Welcome to the human race where everything is part of the global corruptive system set to oppress and exploit others who have all the abundance of natural wealth but are forever in great poverty and corruption.

Fun fact, the British currency is said to be the oldest currency in the world, which is dated back to the 8th century. Did you know that there are between 164 and 180 official currencies in the world today? I bet you cannot name 25 currencies. I would bet that you have heard about US dollars, Euros or British pounds no matter which part of the world you are from. Do you ever consider why?

Africa and other poor nations cannot use their paper money outside their own country. Yet for the countries that are credited with setting the entire global and financial rules, they can use their money anywhere because it is valued and accepted. Is that by accident or design?

To further confuse and corrupt your brain, they come up with numbers and statistics, rules and economic terms that the majority of the world's population do not understand resulting in them turning around and saying, 'Well, that is not for me, I will leave it to the experts.'

They are the experts and that is because they rule the world and set their systems to ensure it is hard to compete with. Everything is designed and made this way, so you do not pay attention to it or give it the time of day. Do you ever wonder why the countries that are rich with natural resources are very poor and always have war, corruption, disease and political unrest?

The global economic game is never set to benefit the majority of people – just look at the rich and wealthy versus the poor and impoverished. For one man to become rich, many others will have to be poor and deprived. For one nation to become rich and powerful under the financial rules set by the big superpower nations, many other nations will have to remain poor, corrupt and unsettled so that they are easier to exploit.

There are over 197 countries in the world but only

a small number are financially rich and powerful, even though more than half are rich in natural wealth.

Africa has 54 countries and none of them belong to the super rich and powerful despite all their natural wealth and potential. When you talk to people about poor nations, people will always say the same thing; they are corrupt. Even most Africans will say something similar. Do you think these nations and their people are the only corrupt ones on this planet? Are they more corrupt than your own leaders and rule makers?

To further develop my point about corruption, please consider who is responsible for the following. Who built and controls the global financial rules and monetary systems, the sanctions and global financial collapse? Who manufactured armaments and wars, colonisation and slavery, and coups in poor countries? Tell me if this is not corruption at the highest level. None of these were set or made by Africans or poorer nations but they receive the blame for it all.

People will make weapons, war planes, vehicles and ships, and sell them to vulnerable poorer nations. These same people sell machines of war yet sit in political conference rooms advocating for peace. They broadcast it on their TV and news outlets stating they are going to aid and help the people, while blaming them for being violent and corrupt. Thereby the citizens support their nations and leaders because they sincerely believe that they are helping the world to be at peace and to become a better place for all. Most people never ask the question; who is making, selling and supplying the war machines, and why? Who starts the war?

One thing I have come to understand in this world is that people never speak about what they take from you, only what they gave you. I call this type of behaviour 'unfair self-proclaiming kindness'. You want people to see you as the good guy, so you keep the so-called bad guy in the dark. This is how the world goes round. They control the media that we watch and listen, and we rarely ask questions because we are all too busy trying to make ends meet. In fact, we are manipulated to remain in a state of 'making ends meet'. Any issues beyond our doorstep are not our problems because it seems there is nothing we can do as ordinary people, despite us caring. We, the poor people, are the majority and while we may seem powerless to the contrary, we are collectively powerful.

We are all living in a corruptive system and a confused world. We would rather leave things to the experts because of how complex and corrupt our laws and systems are. But many of the so-called experts are part of the problem, not the solution.

Corruption is a 50-50 blame game, but unfortunately many people do not see it that way. If you did not realise that corruption in Africa was deliberately taught to the people, then take the opportunity to understand why and how. You have been taught to be politically correct and that everything your government says is the gospel truth. You believe that the news is holy truth, and you put your trust in the organisations and institutions that tell you the Western people who came to Africa did so to help the people. You believe it because you trust them.

Everything in this world comes in twos; there is up and down, back and forth, left and right, happy and sad and so on. When it comes to histories that are being written about other nations' involvement in Africa, the narrative has all been one-sided. Everyone claimed they were there to help the people! The people of Africa never helped anyone. Do you ever wonder why it was never a two-way situation? I am afraid to tell you that this was done deliberately so you do not see the pain and suffering that African people are going through to extract their natural wealth for pretty much free, helping the Western world have a better life. If I told you that hundreds of millions of African people have perished over the centuries, falling victim to the most heinous crimes and tortures against their human rights, what would you say? These same nations are the ones pointing fingers at Africa today talking about human rights abuse and corruption in our continent.

This is not me playing the blame game. This is to help you understand that the people and nations responsible for the treatment of Africa should be held accountable and take full responsibility for their actions whilst resolving the problems they created so we can all move forward. People may say, 'Well, that was a long time ago, and I was not there, and it is not my fault.' It is not the ordinary citizens' fault; it is the fault of your government and their systems along with other organisations and a few individuals. If you are from the richer nations, you may think your country has nothing to do with what poorer countries are going through today. You have been fooled. The world powers and the supremacist individuals have still got their hands on Africa; they have geared their system and laws to keep on biting the poorer nations, keeping them corrupt and underdeveloped so that the corruptors are the ones that benefit.

It is hard when you know people have done so much wrong to you and your people, yet they do not want to take responsibility, and instead try and throw the blame on someone else or the victims of the system. I was talking to someone about slavery, and the person's response was, 'Well, your people were the ones selling their own people.' They did to some degree, but there can only be a market for something to be sold if there are buyers to purchase them. Did you know that Africans did not have guns then? They only had bows and arrows. Did you know that they were torturing the Africans, shooting them to death in front of their families and loved ones? They were forcing them to catch their own people, otherwise their lives would be in danger. You do not think for a minute that these foreign raiders could outrun the Africans in their own jungles, do you? No, they paid and coerced the Africans who had the capability to do the dirty work for them. Let me ask you this, if some powerful people came to you and said, 'help us get what we want or we will rape, torture and murder your loved ones,' what would you do?

Today, we call it 'black on black' crime but you do not see the ones pulling the strings because they are in the dark and remain at a distance. This is how they get into your mind. Corruption itself is a two-way system. Strive to sharpen your senses and hone them to observe things in detail and question everything. Do not let people think for you.

Do you know why no one will mess with Russia, US, China or North Korea? Because they have political, financial and military capabilities. If you mess with those nations, they will come after you. Africa does not have the capability to defend its own borders, people and natural resources; this is why for hundreds of years the continent has been exploited and its citizens continue to suffer at the hands of outsiders.

Everything the news and media feed to you about Africa is negative because that is how they want you to see Africa. They want to keep their dark deeds hidden and direct everyone's attention to the things that keep you thinking that Africa is nothing but a dark continent that needs cleaning up.

Fair enough; I cannot blame them for that because the media is mainly a propaganda machine for the supremacists, after all they own it. History is often written by those who control the narrative and they have always portrayed Africa to be the most corrupt place on Earth. There is corruption in Africa and bribery is rife, especially in my country, Sierra Leone. If you go back beyond five hundred years when Africa was all by itself, you will find that Africa was at peace with no corruption, no wars, disease or poverty. The indigenous people were living in harmony with each other. In fact, if you read African history, you will find that most of the pioneers of modern-day inventions and education started in Africa.

Visit Timbuktu in Mali or the Sankore University and Djinguereber Mosque, which were created around 1100 AD and were then fully established by Emperor Mansa Musa, who is regarded as one of the richest people in history. You will learn that most of what you see today has been developing in Africa for centuries, but you do not hear about this history.

Corruption is not just about people exploiting government money or aid money; it comes in different ways. Through telling lies about Africa, they are altering 'history' and writing their own versions of Africa's past, claiming to civilise and educate Africans when the truth is the complete opposite. This is another example of great corruption and a crime against humanity, providing false history to the wider world about Africa. Corruption in Africa is divided into two categories: internal and external. This is because the negative opinions of Africa have been deliberately directed and taught to the people by those who came looking for natural wealth. That is why there were no records of corruption in Africa before the invasion of the continent.

The other corruptive act against Africa is that the continent's history only started about three hundred years ago, and sometimes is argued to be as early as the 1950s. What some people do not want to accept is the fact that human existence started in Africa before anywhere else on Earth. Africa's history has been active for tens of thousands of years. The colonial powers claim that they discovered everything in the continent of Africa, this is also part of the corruption misleading the people. It is Africans who discovered everything in the continent. They have names for every river, ocean, city and nation, but when the invaders arrived, they changed everything and wrote their version of history stating that they discovered it all.

I was at the Liverpool Museum a few years ago and a gentleman was giving a talk on the history of Africa. He mentioned that some of the first proper toilets were used in Africa, centuries before the Europeans. I smiled and we both cracked a joke about it. I am bringing this up because every time I research and read modern history, all the historians and archaeologists agree that life began in Africa. At the time of writing, the oldest human fossils found were in Morocco dating about 300,000 years old, though the history of human existence on Earth seems to be changing all the time as new discoveries are emerging.

If humanity has existed in Africa for longer than anywhere else, how come when I read about the oldest religions, none of them were founded in Africa? When I search for one of the oldest religions in Africa, Voodooism, which is also practised in many Caribbean countries, Brazil and the US, it is said to be as old as 6,000 years or more yet is still not listed in the oldest religions. How can that be?

When the Western imperialists arrived, the first corruptive strategy of Africa was to change the way Africans think and behave. Most of our native religions were abolished and our people adopted colonial religions, the oppressors convinced the Africans that Voodoo is a satanic practice. Those who brought Christianity and other religions to Africa have tortured, killed and raped millions of our people and that is okay, yet the Voodoo religion that does not carry these kinds of vile records is seen as an evil religion.

Interestingly, if you look at the issues surrounding race today and how African people are disrespected, it is because we always try to be like other people and try to live their way of life. When you try to 'fit in' rather than be true to yourself, how can people come to know the real you? When you mask who you are in order to gain acceptance, why should they trust you? We have abandoned our culture and history; therefore, others often treat us with limited or no respect.

Corruption clearly is not just an internal affair in Africa; it is extended to all the countries that say they colonised the continent. They give a false history about Africa, saying that they took all its natural resources for free, claiming to their people that it was a fair transaction, and now China is carrying on that tradition. They tortured millions of our people to extract natural raw materials for themselves while the indigenous people worked in some of the worst conditions of slave labour ever.

The people were divided and made to hate each other by the imperialists because they found out it was an effective way to extract free resources. They taught some tribes to be clerks and civil servants, teaching them to only think of themselves and no one else. This is one of the worst corruptive patterns in the world today and it is why Africans now behave this way to each other. Africans were taught to take from others and hand it over to their masters, that they should only respect and treat their masters with dignity, even though they were treated inhumanely.

The internal corruption today is mainly linked to the long years of Western education in Africa and to imposing their system of take, take and take again without worrying about others. Hate, bribery, brutality and theft, which were not there before the arrival of the colonisers, are the addictive destructions of our culture today. Slowly our people are awakening, willing to take the right path and understand our history. They are learning that we were once uncorrupted and getting along with each other just fine.

The monetary system and many other laws used to govern most African countries today are set by their colonial corruptors. If any African leaders try to change those laws or constitutions, they are met with the dark side of those imperialist states that will plan and orchestrate coups and unsettlement, or even the assassination of any leader that does not want to comply with the imperialist rules.

Even if the imperialists are not physically involved, they will be pulling the strings from behind closed doors. For example, some African leaders are piling billions of Africa's wealth into European banks. The IMF and many of those crying about corruption know this but they do nothing about it because they are making millions in interest rates every single day. I bet you, when any of those leaders pass away, their money is left in these banks and will never be returned to Africa.

When I spoke to someone about this, the first thing the person asked me was, 'Where is your proof?' I responded by saying that the evidence is available for anyone who is interested in the truth and not propaganda. People cannot always see the truth when they are busy trying to survive and makes ends meet for themselves and their families. It is hard to find time to do the research when your life is devoted to your work and survival. Anyone can find the truth if they are willing to look.

I will finish this section with a story filled with love, hate, racism, and external corruption. Sir Seretse Khama was the first prime minister and president of Botswana. He led from 1965/66 to 1980. He was born into a very influential royal family of the Bechuanaland. He married Ruth Williams, a British white woman, which brought a lot of controversy within the South African national party. It stirred debates among the British and his local people in Bechuanaland. His marriage to Ruth sparked anger with the South African Apartheid government and they put pressure on the British government to agree that he was not fit for office. In 1951, Seretse Khama and his wife were exiled from Botswana. This is just one example of what I mean by external corruption. Exile and assassinations by imperialist states are a big part of the systematic, secretive and behind the scenes corruption that continues to haunt Africa today.

COLONISATION

I will say that anyone whose country has been involved in colonisation should refrain from using that word or telling Africans that we colonised you! For Africans, the true definition of colonisation is to steal, rape torture and dehumanise the locals making them appear as uncivilised animals. This is exactly what colonisation truly is. In the hands of the coloniser who aims to justify his evil deeds, he writes and educates his people that colonisation was a Christ-like experience for Africa. This is also misleading. When the same thing happens to Western nations, it is an invasion, but when it happens in Africa, it is colonisation!

The worst thing that ever happened to Africa was colonisation. It serves nothing else but the selfish interest of Western countries and the oppressors, who have kept Africa far away from its development, culture, religion and freedom to progress towards a better future independently.

European and Asian countries, along with The Arabs and the United States of America have carried out the most inhumane treatment of the black race of Africa. They have reaped all the continent's vast natural wealth, thave tortured its people, have assassinated its freedom fighters and leaders whilst imposing their religions, languages, political rules and capital punishment on us. They have deliberately used propaganda to create stereotypes of backward and violent people unequal to other races. They have achieved this through their media coverage and the education of their citizens.

Today we are experiencing the aftermath of racial discrimination and hate against black people around the world. Africa is left in a dilemma of confusion among its people in deciding which European tribes they belong to, and which religion is right for them. This has caused many internal conflicts among many communities, and lives have been lost due to our misunderstanding of who we truly are and what our real religions were before Western people arrived in our lands.

Nowhere in the world will you find people adapting to African languages or our religions as we Africans have adapted to others. You will find the world's languages, cultures, religions and education systems in Africa, which has left us vulnerable to the influence of corruption. Over the centuries, we have been the most exploited people on planet Earth.

The outside world knows so little about the truth of Africa that even to this day, many stereotypes and prejudices remain. There is very little truth in the history written outside of the continent about Africa. As far as the rest of the world know, Africa only came into existence when the Europeans arrived a few hundred years ago. According to today's history books, the Western people came to help us build our civilisation! Most of the countries and cities in Africa today have names that were given to us when our continent was invaded. Our names have changed and basically everything else has altered because of the Europeans. I am still waiting to find one Caucasian person from Europe called Santigi Bangura! We are still using all the names that were given to us because we too easily accommodate others and their cultures.

In reality, for over 250,000 years, Africa has been in existence. We have had kingdoms with monarchs living luxury lifestyles peacefully with each tribe. When outsiders began to descend upon Africa, our history was reduced to only 300 to 500 years old. The hard truth is that no one came to Africa to help us; they came to steal. When our people began to fight back against their wicked ways, they cleverly told the world that they were giving us our independence!

As much as we are getting rid of the 'N word' and other derogatory language, I must say that we should do the same and completely get rid of the word 'colonisation'. Knowing the history of what the colonisers did in Africa, it always strikes me when ordinary people say, 'So, Sierra Leone, it was colonised by the British, right?' or 'Is Sierra Leone British or French?' Sometimes I will answer what they want to hear because I try not to be disrespectful to those who have been fed an incorrect history. On other occasions, I will say, 'Sierra Leone is neither a French nor a British colony!' The looks on people's faces is priceless!

If the people asking about colonisation really understood the damage and destruction that has been caused, then they would never again ask those questions again. I cannot blame them because the colonisers controlled the narrative and made it sound as if they were there to help the indigenous people. In my definition of colonisation, it says: 'To take for free, to rape, torture, kill, mutilate, corrupt, bully, discriminate and dehumanise the poor people of Africa.' It is worse than the 'N word', and it is not a thing anyone should be proud of.

I found this unknown African quote and I would like to share it with you. It read: "Africa was not poor. They took our gold, our diamonds, and even our people. They robbed us by convincing us that it wasn't ours."

And once upon a time in Africa…

We paid no tax.
There was no starvation.
There was no unemployment.
There was no inflation.
There was no aid.
There was no debt crisis.
There was no unhealthy food.
There was no corruption.

And then the imperialists arrived to 'improve things.' Since then, Africa has been struggling to find its own true culture and way of life. Colonisation did not serve to help Africa but to impoverish the continent and its people.

To give you a perspective of what some of the colonial nations have done, here are some realities and insights into how the modern-day world's brutality is killing the African people and keeping the continent impoverished and backwards.

Britain

The British built their economy through brutal force in Africa since the 1800s. They slaughtered many South Africans when they discovered that the land was full of gold and diamonds (this is why the war with Shaka Zulu started). Apartheid was introduced to the peoples' land, resulting in torture and death for many. In Kenya, the atrocity against the Mau Mau people was one of the worst crimes in the history of Africa. This was for the gain of capital interest and imperialism. They tortured and killed locals so that they would fear them as the imperialists who had forcefully taken their land, enslaved them and brutally murdered many of their family members. It was a similar story in West African states such as Ghana, Sierra Leone, Gambia and Nigeria. Zimbabwe also suffered the same fate. Brutal deaths caused by the British number 500,000 to a million - all in the name of protecting the interests of the British Empire.

Germany

Germany was involved in Africa from 1682 to 1721 when the Brandenburg-Prussia realm existed. The Germans also started in the Gold Coast of West Africa, today known as Ghana, and the establishment of the so-called German Empire worked its way throughout many countries in Africa. In Namibia from 1904 to 1908, the Germans killed up to 100,000 native Herero people who stood against their supremacy, colonialism and imperialism. Their method of attack was genocide, concentration camps, starvation and human experimentation through lethal torture. The German perpetrator of all those brutal atrocities was their no-good general, Adrian Dietrich Lothar Von Trotha. The Germans led a meeting in 1884-5, which is known as the Berlin Conference or the Scramble for Africa, without the knowledge of the Africans. This was done so that Europe could continue its illegal activities in the continent through exploitation and could continue to impose its brutal rules, forcing the people into poverty and enslavement.

France

The French continue to occupy most of Africa today. They are behind some of the most heinous crimes against

Africa and its people. The French army still has a big presence in Africa so that they can protect their capital interests. They assassinated many of the so-called French colonial country's leaders that stood against the French occupation and wrongdoing in Africa through supporting and plotting military coups. They systematically dismantled any government and replaced them with a French puppet so that their inhumane acts and control of wealth continued. One of these corruptive acts is the French government taking over half a trillion dollars from 14 African states for the past 50 years. If you put all that together, it means that over 25 trillion dollars has been sent directly to the French central bank. They let the poor nations sign petitions by people who could not read or understand what they were signing, stating that they must pay for colonisation after they were kicked out of Africa. This is still going on. When a leader says no, they plot a coup against him. The currency CFA is being used by the French Government to exploit some West African states. When Guinea-Conakry said no to French rule, they destroyed the whole country by trashing roads, railway lines, and other forms of infrastructure. Through these inhumane rules, they have caused the deaths of millions and left the people in poverty. Today they are taking all the profit from the oil industries, including profit out of South Sudan where there is so much unrest and civil war. The French army is not in Africa to protect the people as they pretend to be but to protect their chosen corruptive leaders and capital interest.

Belgium

One of the most heart-breaking things is how Africa is seen around the world. When the George Floyd protests took place all over the world, I watched a short documentary about the protest in Belgium in June 2020. The Congolese citizens residing in Belgium were angry to find statues and history being written about the 'dark Africa' and how the Belgians had come to help the people of the Congo. Of course, this was not true at all. The Belgian government has deliberately and continuously kept the people corrupt and poor. I know you might say, 'Well, the Congolese are in control of their country'. Well, that is not the case, and I will discuss this topic later. Watching the documentary was painful because a Belgian veteran was asked about the evil things that Belgians had done in Congo. He believed that Belgium had done well for the people of Congo stating they had helped the people by making their lives better and getting them out of the dark. This man had never set foot in Congo before.

This is where I think the whole world has a big problem with their concept of Africa. People have been educated to believe that their empires have come to the aid of the continent, bringing education and help.

But they have not. They have kept the people and the continent backward and continue to drain its economy and resources. If they help educate the African people and build Africa's economy, then they will not be able to exploit the people. The only people they educate are their clerks, who become their puppets.

During the protests, people climbed onto the statue of the brutal murderer Leopold the Second of Belgium. It is overwhelming as an African to witness a man like that held as a hero in his native land knowing that he slaughtered over 10 million Congolese and looted billions of their wealth. He treated them like animals and enslaved them just to make Belgium a rich nation. Even when they are told that their country is guilty of a barbaric and inhumane act against the Congolese people, they are still in denial and pretend that it was okay to commit brutal killings. Nobody wants to see a statue or photo of someone who tortured and murdered their family or fellow citizens. Yet people said to me, 'It is part of history and people should not destroy statues.' My question was, 'would it be okay to have Hitler's statue in Germany?' You might think that the comparison is unfair but consider for a moment that we view these men how you may view Hitler. Usually I get no reply, but my point is that these countries and their empires and military heads are part of a perpetual lie which is being told to the world. When the truth is out, if people really care about human values and not just their national history, those who committed the atrocities in Africa should not be held up as heroes.

Over the years we have seen how many global 'superstars' have been found guilty of acting on their dark ambitions – the likes of Jimmy Savile, Jeffrey Epstein and too many others. It seems those same criminals had connections at the highest level, high enough for them to be protected from identification.

The higher you go the more the narrative of history is manipulated to protect the guilty. In some cases, histories have not been altered but erased. People who were once regarded as heroes are now almost forbidden to even talk about because the whole world came to realise their dark deeds. But I guess no one said, 'Well, leave them because it was part of history.' Once again, you have to question how all those who have conspired to stay silent or cover up their own part in the criminal acts of such individuals have not yet been brought to justice. Is the answer so blindingly obvious that they control the narrative.

How come people are in denial about the human and economic catastrophe that the Belgian government have caused in Africa? Why are the rules always different when it comes to Africans? It is estimated that the Belgian government killed over fifteen million of our people and no one has been held responsible. The world just let it slide because it is Africa! The Belgians who ruled and controlled Congo have killed more people than the entire population of Belgium. The size of Congo is 905,567 square miles, which makes it the 11th largest country in the world. And Belgium's size is 11,848 square miles, which makes it the 136th country in the world by size. This means Belgium can fit into Congo 76 times. The natural wealth of Congo is one of the richest in the world. How can a tiny country in Europe take over a country in Africa that big? All while torturing its people, paralyzing its economy, and treating the people like animals? Yet nothing is done to get Belgium to return the wealth they have stolen from the Congo even though we know what they did. It does not seem to matter, because the lives of Africans are worth less to the supremacists and they control the narrative.

Portugal

The Portuguese were among the first European invaders of Africa. They were the ones that expanded the enslavement of the African people through the Atlantic. They stole gold and other resources that they traded outside of Africa to build their economy. As we know now, during those slave trade periods, our people were not treated like humans. The brutality towards them was vastly overwhelming to the slaves and their families. Millions of our citizens lost their freedom, dignity and their lives through the abuse of their human rights. We are continuing to suffer those inhumane acts by the

Portuguese and their counterparts in the transatlantic slave trade. When people talk about colonial abuse, the Portuguese do not come into the conversation very often compared to other European nations. It is almost like the Portuguese had done nothing brutal to the continent of Africa and her people, yet they were involved more than most.

USA

When it comes to getting rid of leaders in Africa that stand against the Western imperialists, America has always been a mastermind behind plotting assassinations and supplying the expertise for their European counterparts. America is rarely talked about as a major player in the impoverishment of Africa compared to the other nations mentioned above. The reason is that America holds big purse strings, big enough to be able to manipulate entire governments and distribute billions to control and coerce all players in any given situation. Even when people know some of the things that the US government and their agencies, such as the FBI and CIA, are doing around the world are unacceptable, people still turn a blind eye because there is something to be gained from America.

When Patrice Lumumba (the first Prime Minister of the Democratic Republic of the Congo) was assassinated, research showed that most of the plot was conducted by the CIA and FBI. They were involved in the killing of Lumumba because he was a great African leader who wanted to build the Congo for the good of his people. Patrice Lumumba even begged for help from the US government, but they turned their backs on him. He then sought help from the Russians, and was branded a communist, which gave ample reason for his assassination. Yet no one wanted to criticise the US because of their political and economic affiliations.

In recent decades, under the guise of 'vaccination' programs and 'drug trials', Africans have been used as guinea pigs for what has turned out to be biological weapons with dire outcomes rather than safe pharmaceuticals. If your regime has a bioweapon it would like to test, pick a poor country, bribe some officials, send in a celebrity, big business leader or politician to endorse how you are saving lives, and you are all set.

China

The latest colonisers are now the Chinese. A large cohort of students in Africa are learning Chinese. Our people learn to speak Chinese when they go to China, so the Chinese should do the same when they come to Africa and not just foist their language on us. My hope is that our leaders are now smart enough to not let China or any outsiders harvest our resources and change our culture to please them.

I say we let the real history be our teacher and let knowledge be our power. Do not blindly accept what you are being told. Question everything. Remember this, if you ever ask African people about who colonised them, this is like happily asking someone about who murdered their family member. It is offensive and it hurts. We all must try and learn about the true history and the damage that colonisation has done to Africa.

Spain

The Spanish were equally brutal and took so much from Africa. Just like Portugal, Spain's effects on Africa are rarely acknowledged. If these nations mentioned above were to return everything they took from our continent, they would all economically fall below third world countries.

RACISM

If you have never experienced racism, be thankful. For people of colour, this is something we face more often than you can imagine in every walk of life.

Sport brings so much wealth and joy to countries however it is one of the many stages for discrimination, hate and uncivilised treatment such as monkey chanting and throwing bananas. What is not being taken into consideration is that in Africa we do not treat other people like this. We love, respect and appreciate others: a natural act of civility and oneness. Too many of our people, especially our youth, have committed suicide because of racism. These matters do not make the main news headlines; people are not aware of the negative impact and effect on the lives of those who are racially abused or victimised.

I will share with you my experiences of racism as an African man who has travelled the world.

Before colonialisation, racism was not something that Africans experienced among themselves. Since our existence on this planet, the majority have always understood and respected that everyone's life matters. We have treated strangers with heart-warming welcomes, respect, dignity, sincerity and friendliness. Unfortunately, this is not true everywhere. Simply go back in time a little and you will see where things started to change, where a minority started to act like the colonisers and the supremacists.

We have shared our continent with everyone in peace and harmony except when outsiders were brutal to us. In the past five hundred years, we have been enslaved and raped, castrated and tortured, lynched and segregated in and out of Africa. Our land has been stolen, our natural resources have been taken, our music and culture have been deliberately misinterpreted. To this day, we have been dehumanised to the lowest level; we have been colonised and denied of basic human rights. They have water hosed us, sent police dogs to bite the breast of our women and the flesh of our men and children. We have been denied justice in court and falsely accused of crimes we never committed. Our names have been changed and our ancestors treated as human commodities. We have fought wars for great nations that denied us equality and justice, we have won medals in global sports, we have created the greatest entertainment for humanity while at the same time being discriminated against by other nations. We have loved, cared, shown respect and adapted to different cultures to show solidarity. Over 300 million people have lost their lives through slavery, hate and discrimination. We forgive and embrace people, we cry, we smile, we laugh. We innovate and create goods for the world. We have been whipped, scarred for life, hanged, called all kinds of names. Most parts of the world have looked at us as less than human beings. We have built other great nation's economies, yet we have been denied reparation for what has been taken from us.

Despite all the above that has been committed against us, we have forgiven, and we still continue to give and make this world a better place. There is no record to show that we Africans, since the Moors came to Europe, have committed such inhumane acts against any other nation, race or group of people. Yet we are regarded as the most dangerous and most racist people on earth. We are not racist, we are God's chosen people, and this is why we were first. We have endured more than any other people on this Earth, yet we still love those who have committed these heinous crimes against us.

The African people who are labelled racists are only reacting to the racial suffering they and their ancestors have been through. If you come to Africa as a stranger, you are likely to find a warm welcome, respect and be treated like a king or queen.

It is hard to answer people when they ask us about racism and if it affects us. We experience racism all the time, but we endure it because we are mentally hardened. This is not to say everyone is racist, but it is out there.

BLACK AFRICAN SLAVERY AND BLACK LIVES MATTER (BLM)

"This exhibition explores the history of transatlantic slavery through its connection with the Bank of England and the wider City of London. For over 300 years, the slave trade tore more than 12 million African people from their homes and families. Forced into slavery, they worked without pay and with no right to their humanity, heritage, culture or family ties. In this exhibition, we reflect on how the wealth created through transatlantic slavery shaped the development of Britain".

Slavery and the Bank of England

Bank of England Museum.

Slavery was an economic opportunity for the colonialists. Millions of our strong and smart young citizens were forcefully captured, whipped and put in the belly of a boat that navigated through the rough Atlantic Ocean for months. They had little food and faced whipping every day, sleeping in their own sick and waste while many were thrown overboard and drowned. Those who survived were sold as slaves, going on to build the European and American economies. This act of inhumanity and violence went on for many years before African people began to stand up for themselves.

I have heard people say to me, 'Well Sam, you know, slavery was not just African people. Africans sold their people too!' This is how some people become defensive when a subject like this arises in conversation. I have never denied that there were not others involved in acts of slavery. I am just saying that there is none so brutal and dehumanising as that of our people. Every form of slavery is wrong but all the others who were slaves have had their freedom and mostly equality. Look what is happening in America? A nation built on slavery. Still to this day, many black people are treated like animals through police brutality and social inequality despite the wealth of contributions made to help America to become the nation it is now.

Slavery against African people has been the worst of all. Slavery helped to build Western economies, and today in these countries black people are degraded to the point where I feel that we need to get our act together and build our continent so that we get all the respect that we deserve around the world.

I have seen news reports and videos of police brutality against black youths in US communities and have seen how some of the black communities in Europe are left with fewer opportunities to fend for themselves. All the brave men and women that were supposed to build Africa were taken and enslaved for the development of the so-called great countries. Why to this day do we still have to deal with racism, propaganda, political and social injustice?

The slave trade brought trillions of dollars to the European and US economies, yet after enforced slavery, the great, great grandchildren of black slaves are still facing the same injustice. It is sad that millions of the new generation of black children born in the Western world still face the racism and injustice which their forefathers had fought against. Many things have changed – we do not have to sit in the back of the bus or use segregated toilets – but politically there are still many racial inequalities when it comes to us and other races.

Slavery has done nothing but degrade us and rob us of our humanity, self-worth, respect and dignity. We can change that by coming together as one people who have saved the world through economy, sports and entertainment, education, innovation, peace and love, as I mentioned before.

If mankind's journey began in Africa, then I believe that it was not a mistake for God to choose us first. Religions and societies have turned us into the devil and bad people in the eyes of the Western world, yet we are not the creators of guns and ballistic missiles, nor did we play a part in starting the First or Second World War. We have never invaded or enslaved any continent or people, but we are seen as one of the most dangerous races of people on the planet because the Western propaganda machine has made it so. I want every African to know that the imperialists and colonialists have always had only one thing in mind; to benefit from us and nothing else. Do not be fooled into thinking that Africa has been decolonised – as long as the whole world is there 'helping' us to make decisions, we will never be free or do things independently.

We as Africans have never been part of making decisions in Europe, the Americas, or Asia, but everyone has had their hands on Africa. They pretend to help us while in truth we have been helping them economically through our natural resources. Our slave ancestors fought hard and suffered for freedom and justice, but since it was declared on paper that our people have freedom, things have not changed much politically for us around the world. If it had changed, there would be no need for the protests we have seen in the US and the UK in recent times.

We must change the way we do things so that the blood spilled, and sacrifices made by our people will not be in vain. We are strong with kind hearts and much tolerance, but that is not enough to build our continent and culture. We need to be firm and love each other as one people and one family so that we can stand against corruption and exploitation. Until then, Africa will never be able to stand up for freedom and justice.

No race in this world has suffered and endured the

pain and dehumanisation at the hands of human brutality more than that of the black race. It is always a sensitive and complex topic when it comes to discussing slavery. Why in the 21st century are we still fighting over our people who were shipped out of Africa as slaves and forced to help build other economies and infrastructures? As Africans, we know and respect that all lives matter. Looking at some of the events from the nations that are claiming that every man has freedom, it is clear that they do not practise what they preach. They have been the most abusive when it comes to human rights. This is why I added this topic to help people understand the depth of how slavery is still affecting the lives of African people all over the world.

It was on June 16th, 1944, when George Junius Stinney Jr became the youngest person to be sentenced to death in the United States. At 14 years old, he was executed in an electric chair. He was allegedly accused of killing two white girls, 11-year-old Betty June Binniker and 7-year-old Mary Emma Thames in Alcolu, South Carolina. Their bodies were found near the house where George lived with his parents.

Sadly, George's parents were threatened, prevented from attending the courtroom and expelled from the city. He spent 81 days in prison without being able to see his parents. He was held in solitary 80 miles from his home. All the members of the jury were white; the trial only lasted two hours and the sentence was concluded within 10 minutes. Neither of his parents or a lawyer were present to give him any support. He was so small that most of the execution equipment could not even fit him; he had to sit on the Bible he carried to fit on the electric chair. He had always cried that he was innocent, but hey, these white lawmakers could not wait to electrocute a 14-year-old black child with 5,380 volts on his head! Can you imagine the trauma and nightmare he must have gone through in that prison? Knowing that he would be killed for something that he had not done but was blamed for because of the colour of his skin. Can you really understand the pain that his parents went through day by day knowing that their innocent child would be executed because of his skin colour?

To compound this crime against the boy, his innocence was finally proven by a judge in South Carolina 70 years later. It has been proven that it was a set up to blame him because of his race. Today they still make documentaries about our struggles, but our people are not benefiting from them. They are made by filmmakers whose ancestors have punished and caused atrocities for our people, yet there is still no justice, respect, reparation or change for black people around the world.

And then on May 25th, 2020, 76 years after George Stinney Jr was executed, the internet saw another George being brutally murdered by a police officer with the help of his colleagues in broad day light in Minneapolis, Minnesota, in the United States. A white police officer, Derek Chauvin, kneels on his neck while Floyd is lying face down with handcuffs on. Even when he was begging and telling the officer, 'I can't breathe, my stomach hurts,' the brutality continued. The officer had power, hate, and a heartless soul that would not allow him to have empathy for a fellow citizen that he was supposed to protect, instead continuing for over eight minutes until he died.

As I am writing this, tears are flooding my eyes because I have two mixed race kids that are now seeing how black people are being treated, and they are asking me questions that I struggle to answer.

I posted something on my Facebook page but then I had people messaging me privately to say George Floyd was a criminal, and that he had done this and that. Can you imagine? As if anything would condone police officers murdering a handcuffed man in the harsh light of day. My reply was that it still did not justify why he should be killed when there is a justice system to try him first. Those officers were not working for death row. Given the fact that over 60% of the prisoners in the US are black, it suggests to me that if George Floyd was that bad, he could have been in prison.

People will always be happy to jump to conclusions about others so long as it is not directly affecting them or any of their family members. Just like the truth is always good to tell until it is about you, then your perception changes.

If we think what happened to George Floyd was brutal, can you imagine what happened to his ancestors who were slaves? If he was your family member, do you think it was necessary for the officers to publicly execute?

As much as slavery was for the benefit of the imperialist states, at the same time it was a bigger loss and suffering for their family members and their countries too. In those days, they were only capturing the big, strong and intelligent people, so this is how we lost some of our brainchild of Africa.

And oh, did you know that some of the greatest pioneers, inventors, surgeons and doctors are African or African American? Take a look at the names below and their contributions to our society today.

We have also got some of the greatest scientists who have invented lots of things which are medically known to man today, but these pioneers are hardly spoken about because during the slave trade black people were not allowed to be educated and were kept away from everything to do with progress and development. Take a look at these great people:

Percy Levon Julian, 1899-1975: *Pioneer in the chemical synthesis of medical drugs from plants.*

Philip Emeagwali, 1954: *Inventor accredited with*

the first use of a connection machine supercomputer to help analyse petroleum fields.

Patricia Bath, 1942: *The first African American woman doctor to receive a patent for medical invention.*

Norbert Rillieux, 1806 – 1894: *Inventor and engineer of multiple-effect evaporator.*

James West, 1931: *Invented and developed the microphone in the 1960s. Holds 47 US and more than 200 foreign patents on microphones and techniques for making polymer foil-electrets.*

George Washington Carver, 1864-1943: *An extraordinary explorer and inventor of agricultural science.*

Garrett Morgan, 1877-1963: *Inventor of the first traffic signal and the first patented gas mask.*

Gladys West, 1930: *Contributions to the mathematical modeling of the shape of the Earth, and her work on the development of the satellite geodesy models that were eventually incorporated into the Global Positioning System (GPS).*

Ernest Everett, 1883-1941: *Biologist and author known for his work on egg fertilisation and the structure of the cell.*

Valerie L Thomas, 1943: *NASA scientist who invented*

the illusion transmitter, for which she received a patent in 1980.

Emmett Chappelle, 1925: *Scientist, researcher and a recipient of 14 US patents, who discovered that a particular combination of chemicals caused all living organisms to emit light.*

Abioseh Davidson Nicol, 1924 – 1994: *Medical doctor, university principal, poet, author, and discoverer of the breakdown of insulin in the human body.*

Bennet Ifeakandu Omalu, 1968: *Nigerian-American physician, forensic pathologist and neuropathologist who was the first to discover and publish findings on chronic traumatic encephalopathy (CTE)*

Thebe Rodney Medupe, 1973: *South African astrophysicist and founding director of Astronomy Africa.*

Dr Daniel Hale William: *An African American cardiologist who, in 1893, became the first surgeon to perform successful open-heart surgery in the United States.*

Dr Joseph N. Jackson: *In 1976 he pioneered the TV remote control and several other inventions, holding six patents.*

Many black Africans were recruited in the First and Second World Wars to fight for Great Britain and other nations of Europe, but history does not talk much about them. The same goes for the wars in America where black people (men and women) bravely fought on the frontline, helping to defeat the British. Many were great generals with strategic fighting skills that helped America conquer most of their invaders. But again, these brave men and woman are barely heard of or known today because history has kept them secretly hidden.

To answer people's questions when they do not know much about people of African descent, we are not just people who can run fast but intelligent and gracious people that live on this Earth just like any other race throughout the history of mankind's existence.

During the slave trade, only the strong, wise and healthy were taken, so Africa did not just lose its wealth and natural resources but also the strong men and women who could have built and developed the continent.

When we think we have developed so far as the human race, something pops up that is sadly not surprising to me anymore. At a museum in China, the Chinese photographer Yu Huiping exhibited images of wild African animals comparing them side by side with our African people. It is believed that Africa is China's biggest trading partner these days. Even in the deepest jungles of Africa where they have never seen a TV or read a single paper, they would not treat Chinese people or any other human beings like that. China is now a world super power, so they are telling us that they are more human than us.

China is also the country where thousands of DNA tests were carried out to see if they could trace their ancestors. All the results showed that the sets of Chinese they tested could trace their routes from Africa. But the Chinese government refuted the test and said the Chinese people are not related to Africans. Now they want resources and power – they are all over Africa. Not forgetting during the 2020 COVID-19 pandemic, our people were not allowed to go into restaurants or shops, and there were many videos floating around the world showing our people being disallowed to enter shops and supermarkets, while other races including Chinese citizens were allowed to go in.

In the US, there was a human zoo using black African people like animals. In Belgium, they still have the human zoo of black African people. If people think that Africans are primates, then this is insulting – we have never disrespected any other race of people in history.

I do not personally go around protesting that my life matters, but when you see our people doing it, it is because things have not really changed much since the 20th century. Just because it does not happen to you, does not mean it is not real. In the dystopian future contrived by the supremacists, the colour of your skin will not matter, you and I are their product, we shall both be enslaved. Are you ready to accept that?

INDEPENDENCE

The word 'independence' in the context of African nations has been misleading from the start. Being independent simply means you are able to care for yourself without depending on anyone to help you. Africa has survived this way for thousand years, then came the Western imperialists who saw opportunities and took advantage of the people. They needed our resources, manpower, our land and even our education and civilisation. So here is the twist; how come now everything is twisted, they gave Africa its independence? Africa has and will never need anyone because the whole world needs Africa, not the other way round. Colonisation and independence itself are forms of expressing superiority to cover the evil deeds of those colonial masters.

I do not believe in independence and how it is celebrated and pushed in our faces because Africans were independent before any other race on Earth. Our people need to fight the invaders, imperialists, oppressors, thieves and murderers for what they have done and are still doing to our land and people. We were free from the day that man existed on this Earth, so we must try and abolish the idea that we fought for our independence or that we were freed by those who exploited us. If we want a good name to celebrate, we should rename it as 'Kick

Them Out Day' because this is exactly what happened.

This is only giving more superiority to those who came and stole from us. Our people fought for the exit of the imperialist. We have always been free and independent because we never took anything from others or asked them to come and help us. They needed things from us, so they were the ones that were dependent. They depended on us for raw materials, human labour, education, sports, culture and wealth. We actually gave them their independence to return back to their homelands and enjoy what they had stolen from us.

Someone who is independent does not go to their next-door neighbour and steal their food and possessions. Independent people share what they have with others, which was what Mansa Musa did in the 1300s. As Bob Marley said, "Free yourself from mental slavery." Do not let people write your history for you because they will always be the saviour, and you will be the hungry and desperate servant. I do not celebrate African independence and I think we should all free ourselves from it. If someone brutally beats, rapes and kills your family and you have the chance to fight and get rid of them, you will not celebrate that every year, would you? You surely would not call it your independence!

The first thing that we all must be aware of is that nothing happens in the world of humans without words forming first. Words are critical things, and we need to be careful about the ones we use and the effect they may have. The words you may think are there to make you look great may not be doing so. Words like 'Anglophone' and 'Francophone' are words that are given to us to reinforce who has colonised us. We must reject these kinds of attributes and take off those tags of identity in our society; let us call ourselves what we once were.

Let us take another example, like the word 'government'. If you break it down, you will have 'govern', which means to control, and 'ment', which means the mind, but if you look at Wikipedia today, all the definitions have been changed or altered to reflect Western belief systems. So we know that 'government' means to control the mind of the masses; that is why humanity is struggling today, because we never look deeper into words. A lawyer and a journalist study pretty much the same thing: WORDS. They can use them to manipulate the human mind whether that be through the media and news or to win a killer's case in court and defend the innocent.

So, the word 'independence' to me is like being happy that someone has given you the freedom that was not theirs to take in the first place. Another word for independence is surrender. If you are the coloniser who stole the wealth of a country and you are being forced to relinquish control of that nation, how much nicer is it for your people to hear that you are providing independence to that country rather than handing back what you stole. In common law, each one of us was born free and this Earth is not owned by anyone, we inhabit it together. However today we have to pay for it to the supremacists, those who act like they own it and to whom we owe nothing. My parents are the only people that I recognise who have a justifiable claim to giving me independence.

AFRICA VERSUS THE REST OF THE WORLD

This is a very hard fight for the continent of Africa because it has been divided deliberately by nations from around the world just so that they can build their economies and develop their nations. This is something that started thousands of years ago during ancient times. It all started with the people from southern Europe and Western Asia arriving on the northern part of Africa. They took gold and other precious resources, as well as our culture and education, then they began to enslave black people because we were seen as less than human.

Of course, those that arrived on the continent of Africa were actually coming home where they originated from. As we know the earliest humans were from East Africa. This means that the first humans were black Africans, as they migrated to different parts of the world through various adventures, their human features began to change. I believe that every bit of what we are experiencing today in our modern society began in Africa – education, civilisation and innovation. How come Africa is not known for anything positive in today's world, only negatives like corruption, disease, hunger, wars and being seen as uncivilised and backward? How come Africa's history is only known to the world because of modern-day colonisation which dates back to the 1800s?

I believe it is because all the nations and their people that came to Africa did so to invade, torture, kill, enslave, and loot. Then they went away to build their communities and upon their return to their families or nations all the true stories were twisted so that they would be regarded as heroes in the eyes of their people. This is the mental state of superiority of those who want to control the world through greed and selfishness. Yet Africans never sought superiority, we are a people of resistance with a natural ability for anything created on this Earth. Those who came to gain from us with brutal force decided to dehumanise us so that we would forever be less human to them because of the fear that we are the true people of this Earth by nature. Greed and selfishness from others has turned us into the most dangerous people on Mother Earth. Make no mistake, force superiority exists everywhere around the world against African people. This is a deliberate act of the imperialist who is always fearful that one day Africans will do unto them as they have done to us for centuries.

I am an African first, and I am proud to be black despite all the negatives that can often be associated with it. Black is the devil, black is bad luck, the scariest, the rudest, the wildest, and the most corrupt. So first, I refer to myself as African. Our society has reached a point that if you mention the word black, you can feel like you have committed a crime. Regardless of colour, be it black or white or any of the myriad shades in between, every one of us should be proud, not shy or defensive about who we are. We should not see difference as something to be feared but rather celebrated in every way possible.

I believe in the human race but my experiences around the world have led me to understand that as blacks we may often heavily bear the burden of what came before. There have been tremendous strides forward in so many ways, the legacy of how we have been treated through the centuries is, like a weighty rock, something that we still carry in the hope that we can finally place it on the earth and step away with a lightness of being and in that moment, we will be free to participate in creating a better place for all life on this planet.

The modern-day histories of Africa owe their glory to Europe. Or do they? Well, this is the concept of the European continent. When most people look at us, all they see is how poor and underprivileged we are compared to them. This is not the fault of the people because systematically it has been pursued this way by their ancestors who came to Africa for their own good. They committed so many atrocities and caused so much corruption and killing that it would be most unwise for them to give an accurate account to their people about the inhumane crimes they committed against Africa, because to those so-called colonisers, superiority was a key factor to their wicked ways of dealing with Africans.

The most common words to us are, 'Just go back home', spoken by people who judge where someone must be from by the colour of their skin.

One other thing that a lot of people will tell you when you refer to history to educate them is, 'Please, that was a long time ago and you were not there either.' It is funny how it is always okay for victim nations not to look back at their history however we should deal with it and let it go. Naturally it is not limited to foreign states. Politicians are quick to say, 'It is time to draw a line under this and move on'. Of course, those who committed the crime would like us all to move on but that is more in the interest of the criminal than the victim.

History should not be viewed as fact without first understanding the background and motive of the writer. People are happy to believe the version of history being taught in schools as fact because of the authority of the teacher reciting it. A questioning mind is the most powerful. If the narrative of history being taught has been dictated by those with a vested interest in hiding or manipulating the truth to serve their own ends, then the student is not being taught history, they are being taught propaganda.

I am not saying they do not teach or show the true history of Africa, but it seems to me that it is heavily weighted toward covering up for the crimes of the nations who invaded the continent. As we all know, if a lie is told long enough, that lie can become 'fact' and to the unquestioning mind that then becomes dogma.

They took everything from us, but they left us their religions because this way we too would come to believe dogma and would always seek forgiveness. When it comes to how we are treated, it can be through the most brutal punishment for the pettiest of crime or through turning the 'innocent' into the 'guilty'.

COUPS, ASSASSINATIONS, EXILE, WARS AND GUNS

'I fear not the bullet!' - SPJ

'For those who liberate and worship the gun and its bullet have never understood its true act of unkindness; the destruction it brings to fellow human beings.'

I am still haunted by the desperate voices of young men, women and children. I remember the cries of the frail and the old, begging for the gunman not to pull the trigger. The sound of one gun when a bullet is fired is terrifying, let alone hearing ten, twenty, hundreds or even thousands of them going off at the same time. I have seen birds scared for their lives and dogs barking out of fear. For every single life lost, someone is making a profit out of a gun and a bullet.

It is clear that hundreds of millions of people have lost their lives through bullets in the most dehumanising and gruesome ways, and yet it is legal to make, sell and use them. Some nations have perfected the starting of conflict in order to sell weapons to all parties.

A lot of inventions that were made for the good of humankind have been turned into something that harms us, usually for profit. In the case of weapons, they were not invented for the betterment of society. They are designed for one purpose only, to kill. I have seen war; I have heard gun shots and watched how bullets tore apart human flesh and shattered bones. Sometimes, it takes away life in a split second. However, unlike in the movies, most of those who are shot are not killed instantly but pass from this world in great pain, bleeding to death whilst bearing the thought of 'who?' and 'why?'

I have heard screaming. I have smelled fresh blood. I have seen eyes roll back as the victim takes their last breath, crying for help that never comes. I have watched the eyes of those sentenced to death by firing squads – praying to their gods for mercy, in fear of the trauma they face. Citizens stand aside watching the victim as they say goodbye to this world with the fear of the unknown written across their face. I am clear that 95% of people who perish by the bullet are innocent. Why is it even legal to make and use bullets? We do not need a gun to 'protect' the human race. If all those who have been armed refused to use those weapons, the supremacists and the profiteers would be finished. They only thrive by creating fear and providing a solution to take away that fear, 'That person wants to kill you, here is a weapon to defend yourself.' We see it all the time in news reporting where we are told that two countries are building up for war. The narrative of that news is more often controlled by the very people who will profit from the outcome of conflict, their interest is not to create peace but to divide and get rich.

We need love, sincerity, respect, empathy and care for each other.

Evil is not just hiding in the dark – evil is a part of humanity. It is mostly found in the minority that makes the billions through valuing paper money more than the lives of people.

The thought behind the invention of the bullet is nothing but pure evil. If all victims of the bullet could speak, there would not be enough ears to listen, not enough justice to soothe their pain, not enough books to document their fear and not enough time to tell their grief. Since the dead cannot speak, no one can listen.

I do not fear the bullet, but the human holding the gun.

If It wasn't for the bullet... Martin Luther King Jr, Malcolm X, John F Kennedy, Mahatma Gandhi, Tupac Shakur, Thomas Sankara, Patrice Lumumba and many more freedom fighters would have lived longer to help their people, and many of them may still be alive today.

When I was a little boy in my native country of Sierra Leone, between 1992 and 1997, I witnessed many coups and executions. After the war, I did my research and found out that almost all the weapons used came from countries that are part of the permanent UN council. This confused me; how can these nations talk about peace and human rights and freedom when they are the same nations manufacturing and selling the guns? Then they try to make peace. It just does not make any sense to me. How long would the UN survive if a qualifier for membership was that they must not manufacture arms?

As people, we always blame the ones that pull the trigger as the bad ones. We take it that it was the shooter's fault and their responsibility alone. It is their choice to take a gun and shoot. But on the flip side, we should question the reason for the man who makes the guns and bullets. What was his intention behind creating the gun in the first place? As dangerous as guns are, why would any government allow companies to manufacture them? If no one makes guns and bullets, no one will get shot. If no one sells them, no one can buy them. The only use of a gun is to shoot and kill; neither of these are for the common good.

Most people will say, 'Well, it is his or her choice to use the gun!' Well, if you give people the wrong options and choices, they may use them when they are desperate or mentally out of control. No responsible parent would give their child the choice of playing with petrol and fire, so I would think no responsible representative of the people should give others the choice of using guns and bullets. The weapon manufacturers and the politicians supporting them always use words like self-defence or protection in order to defend the manufacture of arms. But who armed the other party? As for the profit, it is usually gained at the cost of life of the innocent.

I have done a lot of research that shows that many of the coups in Africa are supported, planned and funded by Western colonial or imperialist states to protect their political or economic interests. Clearly these imperial states do not really care about the suffering and lives of other people. As my mum always says, 'We are living in an eagle world, because an eagle will go and kill another bird's chick to feed his own chicks.'

In 2011, the Guardian newspaper published an article titled, 'Africa: a continent drenched in the blood of revolutionary heroes.' It said that between 1961 and 1973, six African leaders were assassinated by their ex-colonial rulers, including Patrice Lumumba of Congo over fifty years ago. Most of the coups you hear about in Africa are orchestrated by the former colonial masters or their agents.

Here are some of our heroes that were exiled, ousted or assassinated so that our continent could be exploited.

1. **Patrice Lumumba** was the first prime minister of the Congo and leader of the independence movement in Africa. Assassinated by firing squad in 1961, age 35. His assassination was carried out by the Belgium secret service, the CIA and their allies.

2. **Kwame Nkrumah** of Ghana, who was ousted

in a Western-backed coup in 1966, in which the British government was highly involved. He was a politician, a revolutionary and the first prime minister and president of Ghana, who led his nation to independence from Britain in 1957. He was by far one of the most influential fathers of Pan-Africanism and the Organisation of African Unity (OAU).

3. **Amilcar Cabral** was assassinated in 1973. He was a Guinean-Bissau and Cape Verdean agricultural engineer, Pan-Africanist, poet, intellectual, theoretician, revolutionary, nationalist and diplomat. He was regarded as one of Africa's foremost anti-colonial leaders. He was killed eight months before Guinea-Bissau gained its independence from Portugal.

4. **Felix-Roland Moumie** was the leader of Cameroon and an anti-colonialist. He was assassinated in Geneva, Switzerland, by an agent of the French Service de Documentation Exterieure et de Contre-Espionnage (SDECE) in 1960, after independence from France that same year.

5. **Sylvanus Olympio** was a Togolese politician who was the prime minister and then the president of Togo in 1958. He was assassinated in 1963 through a coup d'état. He was elected as the first president of Togo after the country gained independence from

France in 1961.

6. **Mehdi Ben Barka** was a Moroccan politician, head of the national Union of Popular Force (UNPF) and secretary of the Tricontinental Conference. An opponent of French imperialism and King Hassan II, Barka was assassinated in France in 1965.

7. **Eduardo Mondlane** served as the founding president of the Mozambican Liberation Front (FRELIMO) who were fighting for independence from the Portuguese. He was assassinated by a parcel bomb in 1969 in Dar es Salaam, Tanzania.

8. **Thomas Sankara** was one of the greatest leaders of Africa. He wanted his people to be self-sufficient in producing food for themselves and using the country's natural wealth to develop the nation. He was not a big fan of the IMF and World Bank policies and loans. He changed the colonial French name of the country from Upper Volta to what it is known as today, Burkina Faso. He was anti-imperialism and gave most of the political offices to women, as he believed that they would create much needed change in the nation. A coup was plotted against him by his friend and comrade Blaise Compaore on October 15th, 1987. He was 37 years old. Further research has shown that the French were the orchestrators of

the coup d'état to take him down.

9. **Solomon Mahlangu** was a 22-year-old South African revolutionary who stood against the Apartheid oppression of his people in South Africa. Black people were oppressed and murdered with no one held responsible. Mahlangu and a few of his ANC comrades were tired and fed up with the racial discrimination in their country by the imperialists, so they took up arms to fight for their rights and freedom. In the end they were captured in Johannesburg after a police officer suspected them of carrying something in their bag. A grenade fell out and shots were fired by the police. Mahlangu was later found guilty even though it was clear that he did not shoot those he was accused of killing. This was all done under the South African terrorism law (created by the imperialists to brutalise the local people who stood up to them). He was executed by hanging in 1979.

When talking about terrorism laws, this is a big slap in the face. How can people come from outside Africa, take over the nation, then segregate the people and banish them from normal life in their own country? How can they torture and kill these citizens, yet when they fight back for their dignity and liberty, they are called terrorists? Who is the terrorist in this case?

One of the statements made in the Guardian reads: 'The loss 50 years ago of this group of leaders, who all knew each other, and had common political project based on national dignity, crippled each of their countries, and the African continent. The effects are still evident today.'

The impact of what has been done to Africa and her people is still affecting us today politically, economically, mentally and socially. When you see Africans and our black people taking a stance with all kinds of riot and protesting, this is because we know why we are suffering today. In many places around the world, things have not changed enough.

I am spending my time to write about the dark history of exploitation, racism, corruption and the torturing, killing and struggles we are still facing today, to help educate those who do not have the time to research or try to understand why Africa appears to be constantly in a state of turmoil. If you feel that I am just blaming others for what is happening in Africa, I just want you to pay more attention and do your own research of how the world is run and what Africans have been through.

The very same supremacists that control Africa control you. They only discriminate one way; if someone can be exploited for profit and power, regardless of ethnicity, creed or nationality, they are automatically the target. The supremacists control the narrative. They create division and peace is their enemy. They manufacture the weapons of war and then create the environment within which those weapons will be used. Today, they are even more sophisticated, they can manufacture disease and provide a solution from which vast fortunes are made. The supremacists do not value anything except what they wish to achieve. They hide in plain sight and control psychological operation units that are vast and they use the mainstream media to control what we read, hear and see.

Those great men of Africa were fighting to liberate their people and their countries from political and economic world dominance of the colonial powers, the US and their neo-colonial leaders, who are in place to feed their own interests. In most cases, the United Nations, which supposedly exists to preserve peace, has failed to protect many of the citizens of this world because of its political affiliations to the big nations who are the permanent members.

The guns used in all the wars since then have all come from Europe, Asia and the US. Despite all the central intelligence that these nations have, they will say they do not know how the weapons are getting in the hands of the wrong people. Winnie and Nelson Mandela along with many of their close freedom fighters were all brutally punished in South Africa because of their stand against injustice in their own country. Malcolm X, Martin Luther King Jr are among the many civil rights leaders who have been assassinated in the US for their stance against racism and inequality.

Patrice Lumumba, Thomas Sankara and many other strong African leaders were assassinated in their countries because they stood up for the rights and justices of their people. These men and women gave their lives so that their people could live in peace and enjoy the freedom which was given to them by God and Mother Earth.

Africa is crying and bleeding. We continue to be punished internally and externally. The words 'human rights' never seem to work when it comes to Africa. I want to let you know that no other race of people on this Earth have endured more brutality, torture, discrimination, and overall unjust maltreatment than us.

We have been exploited, shot, lynched, enslaved and imprisoned unjustly, and the history and true nature of our beautiful culture has been deliberately rewritten as propaganda to be distributed around the world. We are still fighting for our human rights. As mentioned before, our people were denied entrance to restaurants, shops and other public places during the COVID-19 pandemic because of political manipulation of the facts and the simplicity of targeting people because of their race. Despite the struggles and suffering of our people for the past hundred years or more and the deaths caused at the hands of imperialists, we continue to forgive, be tolerant, love and care for others with smiles on our faces.

My message is that, until the real truth of our history is properly told by the wider world, and our frustrations and the pain that we have been through is clearly understood, then racism will be hard to cure.

I believe that we are one human race, we all must make the effort to try and learn about each other's cultures and needs. We must come together as one and help each other honestly and willingly before we can start to make progress and move on to a better, more peaceful and loving future. This will be achieved if we, the older generation, pave the way for those younger than us to make this world a better place for mankind.

Stories That Blow My Mind!

We have many advantages today as technology continues to improve and now it is easier to access things and connect with people all over the world. My friends back home in Sierra Leone added me onto a WhatsApp group. One day in 2017, I received a disturbing video that one of the guys in the group had shared. I opened the video to watch it and to my dismay it was a one minute and fifteen second video of our people dying in the Mediterranean Sea trying to cross over to Europe. All of them had drowned and their bodies were floating like dead animals, washed away onto the beaches of Europe and Africa.

I was angry, sad and full of rage seeing such a video.

Most of all I was angry with our leaders that just let these sorts of things continuously happen to their people without taking action, given the fact that Africa has the resources to take care of its own people. I kept asking myself, how could this be? Why are these kinds of events happening mostly to black people? Why is no one taking these issues seriously? What is the African Union doing to stop these sorts of tragedies happening? My mind was in serious conflict. I just could not work out why we were left to suffer like animals while the whole world went on as if nothing was happening.

A few years ago, I was watching TV when the news came up that some Jewish people had been killed in France. The whole world stood up to mourn for the loss of their lives, including the US president at the time, Barack Obama. Everything was well organised with a clear message to those who were involved in plotting the attack that we are united as one to fight against these kinds of barbaric acts against the Jewish people and their community. Yes, I am all for that too; no human should be killed for who they are or what they believe. But the question is, why do some lives seem to be more important than others? Why is everyone just turning a blind eye to the struggles of African people? Why are the world leaders not coming out, marching and protesting against the suffering and dying of our people in the Mediterranean Sea?

I know you will say it is a different situation, the incident in France was a terrorist attack, and those Africans drowning had freedom of choice and in a sense that is true. That same week, in Nigeria, many people were killed, and their bodies burnt to ash by a terrorist, yet the world's media hardly mentioned it.

Are other races more superior to us? This is a question that I repeatedly ask myself because it seems Africans have no standing when it comes to dealing with our problems. It is almost like God gave us everything but at the same time gave every other race, and some of our own leader's, permission to maltreat us. They keep changing the rules to keep us impoverished yet we still have not resolved how to act in unison or how to be Africans building a united African society.

Everyone is dictating to Africa, but Africa does not dictate to anyone. The imperialists came to our continent and created the rules and regulations to suit themselves so that they could exploit us. They took what belonged to us, changed our religion and education, brought their languages instead of learning ours, and enslaved us when we stood against them. Yet today we still do not have the right to speak or be listened to. Many of those who have never been affected by this kind of treatment will say, 'Well, it is hundreds of years ago so you should just move on, you cannot live in the past.' What happened hundreds of years ago is still affecting us today and will do so for many generations to come unless we speak up and make the changes necessary to help our younger generations' future.

It is easy for others to say you do not have to feel like that because they have never been in your situation. 'Sam, do you ever feel racism?', my European friend asked me. 'Well, it is there, but I do not let it affect me,' I replied, 'I just try to be myself, but sometimes it is hard to ignore.' My friend replied, 'Well you do not have to feel that way because we are not racist!' I smiled and tried to change the subject. In reality, my friend did not want me to feel like there is racism and wanted me to be 'comfortable'. I was comfortable but the reality is that racism is everywhere you go.

Others have never been oppressed like African people, so it is difficult for them to understand that someone can be mistreated because of the colour of their skin or where they came from. You have to be black or African to really comprehend the physical, emotional, and social disadvantages we have been facing everyday, especially in the Western world. Most non black people understand that we are humans too, and that we have feelings like everyone else.

All these torments that continue to swirl around my mind, paired with my experience dealing with people around the world and how they have been educated about Africans and Africa, have led me to question what is going on when it comes to African people's affairs. Then I stumble upon one of the saddest stories of a 14-year-old black child who was deliberately and falsely accused of a crime he had never committed. He was brutally murdered by the same people whom his ancestors had worked and fought to enrich. No empathy, justice, equality or freedom, yet America, the greatest nation on Earth, executes its own citizens for no reason other than their skin colour. This is just one sad story out of millions. I have told his story but please remember his name, George Junius Stinney Jr.

This was one of the most disturbing stories I have ever read in my life! It hurt me so badly that I felt pain in my stomach for weeks and I could not get it out of my head, because I had two kids the same age as George. How could this have happened? Why are these sorts of stories not being taught in our schools? I believe most of the global hate against black people will come to an end if governments around the world educate their citizens about the violence and injustice that has been cast upon us for centuries.

Part 3 – African Leaders and China

INTRODUCTION

Our leaders seem to have found another big brother (China) that is willing to pour money into their hands in the name of developing Africa. Clearly, we have not learned any lessons from our history. They are signing deals that in the long run will only serve the interest and benefit of the Chinese. I am aware that whatever money China pours into Africa, it will not account for what it has loaned. In the end, the Chinese will own Africa for the next two hundred years, because there is the small print that always says, 'If you are unable to pay back the loans, we own your land and all your natural resources for this period of time.' If this happens, which it may already have, then Africans will be stuck for perhaps centuries being ruled and controlled by China.

We usually hear the phrase, 'You give a man a fish, he lives for the day, you teach him how to fish, he lives for a lifetime.' This is the philosophy of independence, but we as Africans do not seem to have grasped this idea yet. All we are doing now is letting our people run away from their homes to seek refuge in other parts of the world. Others from outside Africa will come and catch our fish, take what is best, then what is unwanted will be thrown to us. Why can we not catch our own fish and feed ourselves instead of someone doing it for us?

We are now depending on the Chinese to do everything

for us. Our infrastructure is being built by the Chinese, as if we do not have our own engineers, architects and builders. This makes it look like African people do not want to work. The fact is, if you give everything to the Chinese, then our people are losing, and the unemployment will affect Africa. Our people are some of the most tenacious, strongest and hardest workers on this planet. They will do anything to survive and make their nations great if the opportunities are created by our government. In China, they would not give jobs to Africans and leave their own people to suffer. In Africa, we give the work and ownership to the Chinese with money going out of our economy and into Asia.

We need to improve our education so that it will benefit the younger generation on a wider scale throughout Africa. We have the opportunity to develop an educational system to match or surpass anything the world has at present. We should be innovating and structuring more self-development for our people. We have the natural resources to build the machines, the materials to build the roads, the engineers to design and construct our bridges, hospitals, schools and universities. We should have the education to train our own doctors. We should have the economy to pay for their services and a higher standard of living so that they will stay rather than leave their nations and people to suffer and perish. We have the resources to develop our own science research labs and not let others make and manufacture medicines, to dictate how the world works for us. We should be able to do all of this. We are the ones showing others that they are superior to us; this mentality is one thing that we need to change. We must start believing in and trusting in ourselves.

For three hundred years or more the Western world has been in our midst, but nothing has changed or improved for us. We have not benefited from their presence and have ended up in unnecessary debt.

We have always adapted and danced to everyone else's beat; it is about time we created the beat to which we dance. Before we can do that, we need to be ready to change our mindset, but this can only be done when we have great leaders who are willing to make the change. A nation and her people will only be led to a greater future if the leaders are willing to move their people. If our leaders are not influenced by outsiders to be corrupt and self-serving, then Africa will begin to rise up for a greater future. We need to mine our own resources with our own machines, educate our younger generation to build their nations to stand strong against corruption. We should not want to run away from our beautiful Africa. Until we can do these things, Africa will never be independent, and peace and freedom will remain elusive.

INTERNAL CORRUPTION

I have said before that everything in this world comes in twos and this is no different with corruption. You have the external corruption; this is the influence of others from outside that have interest in your society or country. Any type of corruption is a selfish interest by a person, company or government and institutions. So, interest is the reason for corruption, which means the one who corrupts does not care about others.

The external corruption will come in and create divisions between people, influencing them to be selfish and only think about themselves. This is what I call the brain of the corruption; even though it is coming from outside, people do not really see it because the influencers always position themselves to look like the angels and saviours of others (the devil acting like an angel). Internal corruption is the one people usually sense, see or feel the effects of. This is because internal corruption is nearly always in plain sight. When you go to Africa, you can see corruption everywhere because it is not hidden, so this is why everyone calls Africa corrupt. In the Western world, corruption is done secretly and behind closed doors. Their corruption is done educationally where the citizens accept it without realising it is corruption. For example, an insurance company in England will give you an agreement document to read and sign, and all the things that are in your favour will be in the big print, but the ones designed to catch you out will be in the small print. Great news, you are fully insured… until you claim, and they refer to clause Y paragraph 3, sadly it appears you are not covered for the way the damage happened. That should be described as a corruptive act as it is a trap made to catch the unwary. How bad do you feel when they ask, 'Did you not read the full document?' The government knows it and so do the people, but everyone will sign it and accept it as part of the system. That is why when you have problems with insurance, they will always ask if you read the small print. Now every rule and law used in our system in Africa is based on the colonial masters' ways of governing their countries. Our judicial system was not designed by us, it was dictated to us. It is a system that does not necessarily favour the innocent but instead favours those who can afford to pay the most.

After the external corruptor has influenced the internal, he will sit back and laugh through the commotion and state how something should be done about it. Often, they will have the solution ready to sell to the government to protect the people from the corruption they installed and make sure it continues.

Half of the corruption you see in Africa today has been carefully and deliberately orchestrated by the colonial invaders, so their neo-colonial puppets are now carrying the traits that have been instilled in them by their masters.

In colonial times, the clerks were trained by their masters and given the power to brutally discipline their own people through beating and imprisonment. They were taught to hate other tribes and treat them like slaves, forcing them to perform labour without pay. The clerks would show no sympathy or empathy for their people. The police were also trained that way. The imperialist's job was to take, torture and kill anyone who dared to get in the way, without giving a damn for the individual.

After hundreds of years of this corruption, this is what we se today all over Africa. Prior to the arrival of the imperialists, Africans were fine with each other using a barter trade system. They also introduced tax on the people for their own lands, homes and work. In Sierra Leone in 1898, the Hut Tax War was fought by one of our heroes Bai Bureh, who was a general and war strategist. When most of the chiefs in the country signed a petition against it, the use of force by British officials was passed to arrest Bai Bureh. Passing tax law on the local indigenous people for the benefit of imperialist government, whilst arresting those who were strong and educated to fight back, has to be at the top of the list of corruption.

Bai Bureh was captured and sent to exile in Ghana on November 11th, 1898, with two of his fellow chiefs. Bureh was brought back to Sierra Leone in 1905 and died in 1908. This is what is killing Africa to this day. Many years of external corruption has become the greatest disease of Africa. Before the British took over Sierra Leone, people were living in peace with each other, then outsiders imposed their rules and got the people to hate each other (divide and conquer) for the benefit of the British Empire.

What did external corruption bring to us? Force and aggression, hate and division, stolen goods, and laws for the oppressors. This is what you see today in Africa. Our leaders are pouring money into foreign banks leaving their people to suffer. They will torture, divide and mislead the people as part of the imperialist law of becoming rich and powerful.

In 1994, we saw that same internal hate rage in Rwanda by devils like Theoneste Bagosora and Felicién Kabuga, and many other Africans who turned against their own people and severely brutalised them. I am not saying the act of these evil men against their people is solely to be blamed on the imperialist example, but in the history of our continent, the rule of power, hate and control owe some influence on colonial ideology because most of the atrocities started when outsiders arrived and needed the population to comply. There are people who grow to be evil by their own default, but there are also others who are greatly influenced by corruption.

Bribery is one of the epidemics in most African countries today. Too many government officials, organisations and individuals make a living through bribery while seeing the damage it is doing to the vast majority of their people. Sierra Leone is one of the worst places when it comes to bribery. You cannot go anywhere, nor do anything, in the country without bribing someone. It is so entrenched in the heart of our people that is has become the normal way to not only become rich but for many the only way to survive.

It is hard to get rid of corruption today if we do not learn when and how it started, and how it affects more people in our society. If we can eliminate internal corruption among ourselves then it will be harder for the external corruption to take hold of our society. The only way to do that is to first stop being selfish, and instead to love and care for our communities, to think of Africa first, and to unite and care for others. I have repeatedly said that we have to change our mindset and improve our educational system across the continent. Both corruptions are eating us alive and putting almost a billion people in extreme poverty, while at the same time we are empowering and enriching the very same imperialist states that have held us in this position for hundreds of years.

LOANS

Loans are traps to enslave you and your country, especially when they are coming from the same people who have corrupted and unsettled your life and your nation. The best wealth to have today is gold; as Robert Kiyosaki calls it, 'God's money'. Africa has an abundance of 'God's money', yet our leaders have been taking trillions of dollars in loans for over 50 years and nothing has changed that much. The larger the amount, the easier it is to skim from the top and hide how the money is being distributed or to simply lie about where it has gone. The fascinating truth is that the countries that are lending the money will not stop because that is the way they continue to control the wealth of Africa since the colonisers were forced out.

Cleverly, they came up with many ideas, laws and systems that gave the colonial masters the power to dictate and make decisions for Africa. I thought Africa had gained her freedom and independence from the colonial states, but the supremacists found new and more complex ways of keeping us in chains.

Africa owes between $350-450 billion to the rest of the world through loans that were given to our governments as investments for infrastructure and human development. So, how can Africa have tons of 'God's wealth' yet owe the world so much money? Why do these countries keep on lending to our leaders if they do not see any development?

It is estimated that in 2019, Africa had a GDP growth of 3.7% and a total of $2.6 trillion (nominal), 'estimated at $6.7 trillion'. GDP per capita for 2020 was $1.970, which ranked Africa as 6th in the world.

According to studies, in 2013 Africa was identified as the poorest continent. However, that same year it stated that Africa had the second fastest growing economy in the world. So, if the numbers are all in our favour, how did we end up with so much debt? Can Africa pay back the $350-450 billion?

Here are some statistics for Africa from 2017 to 2020:

Nations = 54

Population = 1.3 billion plus

GDP = $2.2 trillion (nominal), 'estimated at $6.7 trillion'

Growth = 3.7%

Top 10 Richest Countries in Africa by GDP

	Country	GDP	Natural Resources Export
1	Nigeria	$446.543 Billion	Cocoa beans, petroleum, crude, refined and gas chemicals, vehicles and aircraft parts, rough wood.
2	South Africa	$358.839 Billion	Gold, diamond, platinum, iron ore, coal, metals and minerals, machinery and equipment, motor cars, agricultural food stuffs, wine.
3	Egypt	$302.256 Billion	Crude oil and petroleum products, cotton, textiles, agricultural goods, metal products and chemicals.
4	Algeria	$172.781 Billion	Natural gas, ammonia, petroleum products, petroleum.
5	Morocco	$119.04 Billion	Fertilisers, petroleum products, citrus fruits, vegetables, fish, clothing and textiles, automobiles aircraft parts, electric components, inorganic chemicals, crude materials.
6	Kenya	$99.246 Billion	Fish, cement, horticultural products, petroleum products, apparel.

7	Angola	$91.527 Billion	Diamond, timber, cotton, coffee, crude oil, refine petroleum products, sisal, fish and fish product
8	Ethiopia	$91.166 Billion	Gold, coffee, oilseeds, qat (Khat), leather products, live animals.
9	Ghana	$67.077 Billion	Gold, bauxite, manganese ore, diamond, oil, timber, tuna, horticultural products, aluminium.
10	Tanzania	$62.225 Billion	Gold, coffee, cotton, cashew nuts.

I am not an economist but looking at all the natural wealth from these countries and their GDPs, along with the fact that we produce more than 30% of globally required resources, how can Africa be the poorest continent? Why can Africa not pay back its debt? Will Africa ever take full responsibility for itself? We can never stand on our own feet and direct Africa's future if we have leaders who are taking endless loans and misusing them for their own selfish reasons, leaving masses of Africans impoverished.

Aliko Dangote is the richest man in Africa, worth over $10 billion. He started his business after borrowing money from his uncle and turning those few thousand dollars into billions. So my point is, yes, loans can work and be helpful if put to good use. If not, a person or a nation is in great danger of becoming enslaved.

Once a person or a nation owes someone a debt and cannot pay that back, then the small print on the agreement becomes an advantage for the lender, and the recipient becomes a silent fugitive spending decades trying to survive and pay them back. In some cases, by the time they settle the loan, life has passed them by.

In my opinion, Africa does not need to take loans or sign large, long-term deals for a short-term benefit. We have all the natural wealth and money we require. All we need to do is make sure our leaders are accountable and use our resources for the development of the continent. Historically, we have had a wealthy, naturally blessed land with an abundance of resources. It is harder for us to move forward as a united Africa because of how wars, coups and political unrest along with European colonisation (as well as some of the challenges created by decolonisation) have created an environment of poor education and economic and social instability.

Yes, I believe we can pay off the loans and be a debt-free continent if we unite as one people. If we can do that, then we will be economically self-sufficient, which will lead to our future of everlasting freedom, dignity and sincere independence. The lenders of course do not want us to unite for it is in maintaining a division of the people and nations of Africa that they keep us in debt.

So once again I say onto Africans, let us either stop

the loans or make better use of them and be a debt-free continent. The IMF, World Bank and the Chinese are happy to keep us in debt because by doing so, we are obliged to allow them to control us and our future. We do not want to leave an Africa that is so damaged that our younger generations will be in debt for the next 200 years.

POVERTY

When you hear the name Africa, the word poverty comes to mind. You do not have to look far to see messages on TV or in service stations along the stretches of European highways that advertise for donations to help our people. The great human spirit to help others is very clear to me, I sincerely believe that the ordinary citizens of this world do care about their fellow humans. The trouble resides in misguided education and the way that leaders teach their people that Africans are corrupt. Those that care to lead their people out of poverty and away from corruption are often overthrown with support from outside vested interests, before being exiled and accused of being a communist or some sort of mad person, sometimes ending in an assassination.

Superiority and indoctrination have led to a wide range of racism everywhere. Most of the images I have stumbled upon in public areas and on TV only serve to make Africans look like people who are unable to take care of themselves. This endorses the impression that everyone in Africa is living in slums, deserts or jungles and has a primitive lifestyle. Of course, we have overwhelming numbers living in poor conditions, but that is because some of our leaders and their colonial allies are deliberately keeping the people that way so they can get away with their illegal activities.

A part of me is happy that people around the world are showing care for others (showing the truth about the human spirit) but the other part of me feels ashamed and angry at the images because that is not a true likeness of Africa and her people. When I travel throughout the US, I see examples of poverty worse than in many places in Africa, but those images are rarely seen on TV. If our people in Africa saw that, they would never want to go to the US. But all you see about the Western world is the Hollywood version. Yes, there is poverty in Africa but also elsewhere on this planet. Yet, many people think of Africans as the most begging people on earth.

I was driving from my little town of Southport in England to London and made a stop at a service station. The image over a urinal was of a young African girl and the message read that the young girl could not afford sanitary pads. This charity was asking for a few pounds in donation to help girls like her. As an African, it is embarrassing to see this kind of image representing our people all over the world. It is like we Africans are now the global charity case. I saw the same in Spain, Germany and the US, advertising for lack of drinking water and kids going blind from eye infections. The point is, how can we expect the world to respect us and treat us with equality when all they see are these kinds of images? Do not get me wrong, the recipients of those donations will be most grateful, often it can be life changing. However, those images are just one facet of a multidimensional continent and do not represent fully and truly who we are.

Images are an easy way to educate people because our brains are very responsive to the likeness of any image, especially when they are photos of people looking impoverished, malnourished and facing a lack of care by their own people. We do not see these kinds of images depicting other countries floating around Africa! No, they do not show us that because they want to keep their dignity. Of course many countries in the world face similar issues, but the difference is that these countries do everything they can to control the media narrative as to what is presented to the rest of the world. But you get the sense that some of those countries do everything they can to minimise the volume of media inches given to that one aspect of their society and culture. We Africans seem to be OK with a simple negative view of what our continent is about. Where is our counter-narrative? Where are the profiles of thriving cities or successful people? Where do we show Africans helping our own?

The image of Africa is so bad outside of our continent to the point that when you speak about coming to Africa to African American people for example, they will look at you like you are crazy because of what they have been fed about the continent.

Yes, many of us along with the charities are out there

trying our best to give a helping hand to those who are struggling in Africa. But at the same time, we should be striving to give a more honest, truthful, and accurate view of our continent and the power to do so in this 21st century. People will only treat us with equality and respect when they know and can see that we are moving forward and are not only aware of challenging circumstances within our communities but that we are doing something about it.

One might think that poverty, like many things happening in Africa today, is only the result of corrupt African leaders. African leaders are corrupt. Well, that is part of it, but the poverty you are seeing today has long been due to the colonisation rules and regulations set in the past. For example, France taking over half a trillion dollars from 14 African nations each year, and also setting lending rules of over 12% to borrow their own money back! This is one of the reasons why Africa has been this way for such a long time.

You may well be thinking, 'Well, here he goes again blaming colonialism.' But it is true, and it was set this way. As Africans, we have been the easiest people to influence and control because we have just accepted whatever has been given to us. Look at the way that Africans and black people in general were treated in Africa during the Apartheid. They came from Europe, took the people's land and tried to convince the people that they had been in Africa for as long as the black people. They tortured vast numbers of the population, took over the government, killed civilians, then denied our people equal rights and justice and segregated them. The same thing happened in Europe, America and other parts of the world, yet today we still do not hold anyone accountable for all the theft and atrocities caused against us in Africa.

No other people or continent would take these levels of treatment without starting a major war. Only Africans can have that level of resistance and still let it go. The prices for our resources are not set by us, the owners, but by the very same people who have been taking all our wealth. Therefore, the result for us today is dependency and poverty. Imagine someone enters your home and declares that they are the new owners, saying they want to make your life better. As you now have no assets, they will lend you just enough money to survive and for that they will charge you 12% per annum interest for as long as it takes to repay the debt that you did not have before they arrived. How is that working out for you?

In today's economic world, for one man to be a millionaire, hundreds (if not thousands) have to go poor. The system of banks giving money out and people making money from each other is nothing but a monopoly system. So long as this system is in place, only so many people will be rich. Just look at the world population and ask yourself, how come there are not many rich people compared to poor people?

It is simply because rich people take from the masses. This is the way that rich people and nations become richer, and why the distance between the poor and rich is ever widening.

Africa has fallen under the grasp of this monopolistic system for hundreds of years. Behind the scenes, everything is controlled by colonial masters who are always pulling the strings that are keeping Africa impoverished. The majority of people in this world cannot see these strings. Those hidden in the dark are the richest people who control 99.9% of the world's wealth. They own the banks, the media, the big tech firms and the pharmaceutical industry. They are the governments and their allies, the corporations and organisations that hide in plain sight. They are the billionaires who should be the face of the beneficent but who are using their wealth with evil intent. Whoever they are, they are all in it together, and they spread their tentacles in all directions so that they can reach all corners. The Chinese are getting blamed more and have been called corrupt because they are also reaching out their larger tentacles to take ever bigger slices of the African cake of 'free' natural resources. Those who have been enjoying it for the past century do not like that.

The African leaders and freedom fighters who have tried to cut those invisible strings have been tortured and assassinated. It is sad for me to tell you that the poverty in Africa today is deliberately kept that way by most of the African leaders, who are supported by their colonial allies and the colonial states themselves. Most of the Western world would likely be third world countries if it were not for stealing the wealth of Africa. There is so much corruption and deep secrets behind the impoverishment of the African people that if one is to understand it, you would have to dig deeper than you ever wanted to. Most people do not have the time. The easiest thing is to believe the Western media, which is controlled by the same circle of people who tell us that we have to pour X amount of money into Africa and that the African leaders are corrupt and misusing the funds. This media forgets to mention what the Western world is taking out of Africa. No one will continue to loan that sort of money to Africa if they are not making a profit or benefiting in the grab of natural resource. You have to use common logic; no one would do business like that, plain and simple.

Should Africa rise to become the world super power it could easily be, many current developed countries would certainly see a negative impact on their economies. However, some of the emerging technologies such as electronic banking, bitcoins, and other so-called breakthrough advancements might contribute to keep Africa impoverished as it struggles to catch up. Colonial states are now seeing that today's young generation of Africans are waking up, so they are now calculating the advantages that Africa will have in the future. The West is racing ahead with all kinds of technologies that will enable them to maintain their power and superiority over Africa and many nations around the world. Africa needs more than just to keep up, Africa needs to set the bar higher.

The Western world is enjoying wealth and a strong economy today because of the impoverishment of Africa. You keep the continent corrupt and poor, and you are able to exploit the people. I laughed when I first heard the words 'blood diamond' because almost every diamond that comes out of Africa, from either a war-torn country or a peaceful country, has some bloodshed behind it. Africa's diamonds are always going to be blood diamonds until we take proper control of mining and distribution. It is simple: if the super world powers do not want blood diamonds, then they should not make and sell the weapons that are taking the lives of the slaves who are digging for things that will sparkle in the windows of Bond Street, 5th Avenue and the Place Vendôme. This is a double whammy – sell the weapons and get the natural resources! It seems that no nation or business will ever say no to a diamond even if they know that children have died for that one piece of a gem. The phrase 'blood diamonds' will never make a difference for the poor Africans who are dying every day. Big Western corporations seemingly do not give a damn about poor people dying.

Why are they called blood diamonds? They are called blood diamonds because they come from communities of conflict. Who do you think manufactures and sells the guns? Well, that is my point. Where do all the blood diamonds end up? Poverty will continue in Africa until Africans cut those strings behind the scenes and unite to create a currency that will surpass any other on this planet. By using our own African currency, we can sell our own natural resources at the prices we choose and let everyone else come and buy them from us.

I know only too well that there are challenges to achieve all this. For now, we do not have the military capability to safeguard and police our countries. We have let many big nations build their bases in Africa, while monitoring our behaviour and how we do things. I know that it takes great courage to stand up to attempt to empower our people, the risk of being killed by those with a vested interest in maintaining the status quo is high. Internationally sponsored state-based murder can be done without the people having knowledge of it, or if we do know about it in advance, we may still be powerless to act. Often those behind the assassination will not cover their tracks so that such action is broadcast as a lesson to others.

We must begin to unite as many of our great heroes

and freedom fighters have done before. We must do this by every means necessary; not to hate others or push them aside but to do the things that will bring us development, control of our future and make Africa the greatest place on Earth. We cannot continue to say it is a pointless attempt; we already know that they will do all they can to prevent us taking power and sovereignty. Yet we must fight to be the designers of our destiny. We must move now before it is too late. We have everything to empower our continent and our people. We must stop being used and take this time to decide what is in our own interests instead of fighting over the scraps off the table of our colonial masters.

Today, we have enough capacity to eliminate poverty in Africa and change the images that are making us look like careless, primitive and uncivilised people.

Our education is based only on theories and not practice. An example of this is that we learn to operate a machine but not to manufacture the machine, because some Western or Asian company has opened a factory and employed the African people to provide the hard labour. We can take injections from someone else, but we are not manufacturing and producing the medicine. We are told how safe these injections are without truly knowing what we are being given.

We study Julius Caesar and the Roman Empire, but we forget that we have our own great history dating back thousands of years. We have great empires like Mansa Musa and great heroes and warriors who have fought for Africa (yet other empires sound more superior than ours). I am not saying we should not learn about others, but we should focus on our own history and things that will benefit and develop Africa. It is in the interest of the world that Africa should become a self-sufficient continent of peace. Unfortunately, it is not in the interests of the financial supremacists, the arms manufacturers and all those former colonisers who owe us so much.

Brothers and sisters of Africa, no one is superior to you. The future of Africa is in your hands. The younger generation and our leaders need to create the path and show the way. We watch our musicians trying to dress and act like musicians from the West. We adopt their cultures while ours are dying. Our young people are being coerced to believe there is something better elsewhere and that they should aspire to chase it. I say to you again, do not change your culture to please others. Be proud and appreciate who you are and where you are from.

When a lot of Africans travel the world, they quickly change and act as if they forgot who they are. They no longer dress and act like Africans. They now eat pizza and McDonald's to look like they are better than their fellow country men and women regardless of the fact that western fast food is manufactured to be addictive and extremely unhealthy. Fufu and eba (a West African dish made from cassava/plantain) may be their passion, but I am yet to see in where they are lining up for our fufu and eba in the West! This will not happen because they want to 'fit in'. Please change your mindset and begin to think like Africans and put Africa first.

Lack of one's historical knowledge and understanding of our rich cultural heritage also plays a big part in exploitation, which is one part of the cause of wide-scale poverty that we experience in Africa today. When you do not have an anchor from knowing where you come from, it is easy for others to manipulate where you are going.

Part 4 – Coloniser's Influence on Africa

Africa is still negatively influenced by its past colonial masters. I am talking about power and resource influence. The colonial states still control the way most African nations are governed, thereby maintaining a hold over the decision making that guides our direction of travel. The behind-the-scenes support for military coups and some of the violence in Africa has led to the exile or assassination of leaders that oppose imperialism and foreign intervention that is shaping Africa's future.

The constitutions and laws of many African nations are set and implemented by colonial masters, and the judiciary systems are all based on what has been given to us. Many of our elections are influenced by the Western world because they prefer leaders that will bow down and collaborate with them. In 1996, the late president elect for Sierra Leone, Dr Amed Tijan Kabbah, worked for the UN but the majority of people did not know who he was or what he was doing. But all of a sudden, he turns up and becomes the leader of the nation. He was ousted by a military coup in 1997. However, he was then backed by the whole world to be reinstated to power, despite the suffering and death of tens of thousands of innocent people in the name of a democracy that does not exist. Was it worth our people suffering and dying just to bring one man back into power that was pulling the nation to its knees? He was backed by the same superpower and when he got back into office, the country became ten times worse than it was. But again, the financial supremacists do not care about the people perishing in their millions, only their own self-interest, continuing to influence and pull the strings of the puppets.

For me, no human life is worth shedding for a democratic system that only exists on paper and in the media; it is practically an illusion to make humanity believe that there is a fair system in place. That fair system will not exist until 70% or more of people in this world realise that we have been lied to. If democracy really exists, it seems that the world would be a more peaceful and better place without poverty and fewer diseases.

Speeches and Quotes from Great Pan-African Leaders, Freedom Fighters and Activists

For those of you who have never faced the horrors of what Africans around the world have endured at the hands of other global citizens, you need to understand the reasons behind the pain and suffering. These men and women speak from the reality of what they have faced and often the bitterness in their hearts about the way Africans and others are treated. You should study the unfairness of the policies, exploitation and brutality that we have exchanged for the goods and resources that we have given to the world. There is a long list of heroes who have fought for their people's freedom; many of them lost their lives trying to uphold their beliefs for equality against the very same people who have pretended that they care about the development and well-being of African citizens. I mean governments, unions, and organisations who are continuously doing everything they can to keep Africa impoverished. I pray that you are fortunate not to experience such manipulation by those who do not have your interest at heart. Unfortunately, in this world today, no matter where you are, no matter your colour, creed or nationality, unless you are truly awrae of what is happening, then it is likely that you are indeed being manipulated. You just may not see it yet. With most of the world's mainstream media being owned and controlled by a small number of very powerful people, we are being fed only the news that suits their agenda. It used to be that investigative journalists would track down a story and tell it regardless of vested interests but now advertisers hold the power. If you are a pharmaceutical giant spending millions on advertising in a national paper, the reader is unlikely to ever see an unfavourable story about that manufacturer's drugs. Sadly, it is too rare to find an investigative journalist who is not willing to alter or bury a story in order to protect their job.

We have a short historical reminder from Professor PLO Lumumba, a Kenyan lawyer and motivational speaker, in one of his speeches in South Africa. He reminded us that our continent (Africa) is not at ease economically. Our continent is not at ease with our health. Our continent is not at ease in our education. We live in a great continent which has great prospects but is now in monumental difficulty.

"*Those who spoke before me had the occasion to narrate to you how we were enslaved and commodified by the Arabs. The Arabs' colonisation project was a project not only of Islamisation but also a project of Arabisation. And when the Arabs were done with us, the Europeans tribes came; if it was not the Portuguese, it was the Dutch; if it was not the Dutch, it was the Italians; if it was not the Italians, it was the French; if it was not the French, it was the Germans; and if it was not the Germans, it was the English. We are victimised; this is our history. This is the only continent (Africa) that has welcomed every civilisation.*

"*We started with the Arabs; we welcomed them, and they abused us. Then came the Portuguese; we welcomed them, they abused us. Then the Dutch came; they abused us. Then the Italians came; we welcomed them, they abused us. Then the Germans came; we welcomed them, they abused us. Then the French came; we welcomed them, they abused us, and then came the English; we welcomed them, they abused us.*

"Then the Indians came; we welcomed them, they abused us. The Lebanese came; we welcomed them, and they abused us. And now the Chinese are coming; we are welcoming them, and they are abusing us. And when slavery had lost its way, some from within their rank pretended that they were abolishing slavery, then they introduced yet another thing, a thing called colonisation. They came to our continent and claimed that they had discovered us.

"They came, and while we were here, they discovered the Cape of Good Hope. They discovered us, they claimed. While we were here, they came and pretended to discover all the lakes and rivers: that is how they came. While we were here, they came and pretended that we had no history, but let us assess history, if only to demonstrate to ourselves that the African continent is the cradle of human civilisation. You know, when Europeans were still living in caves, the Dogons in Mali had already recognised the stars. When the Europeans were still eating raw meat, the Africans had discovered fire. The Africans were the pioneers. Even if you look at all religions and their creation, and I am a keen reader of the Bible, and the Bible records that God said, 'Let us create man in our own image.' And that he took soil and formed man out of it. The last time I checked, soil was brown or black, not white.

"And I can confirm that I checked this morning, the

soil is still black, the soil is still brown, and if therefore anybody is created in the image of God, it is we who are of the black race. Islam also says the same thing. You know Africa has been abused when you look at the maps that are drawn by European cartographers. Africa is smaller than the United States of America and yet is larger, almost as large as Asia. They make us feel small all the time."

Then, PLO went on to say that, *"Despite the fact that they have done everything to erase Africans from the face of this Earth, even in their own history, they acknowledge that all their great men came to Africa – why? And what did they come to do to Africa? Socrates was in Africa; when he came, he met Orunmila of the Yoruba tribe, who was a greater philosopher than him. Pythagoras was in Africa – what did they come to do in Africa? You pay homage where knowledge resides. Moses was in Africa and was born in Africa; what did you come to do in Africa? You pay homage where knowledge is. Muhammad was in Africa; why do you come to Africa? You pay homage where knowledge is. Christ or Yahshuah was in Africa; why did he come to Africa? You pay homage where knowledge is. The lord Krishna of the Hindus was in Africa; why did he come to Africa? He came to pay homage to where knowledge is. This is the cradle of human civilisation. But we have been so beaten over the years, we have been so abused over the years. They enslaved us because they feared us, they colonised us because they feared us.*

"They now have a new project, the neo-colonial project. And I am told that the neo-colonial project is a twin of another child called colonisation and their mother is imperialism. And imperialism never changes his character; it only changes the mask that it wears. We must be wary of it. It is said when they came here and brought Christianity, they told us to close our eyes in prayer and when we opened our eyes, the land had disappeared. That is who they are: they are not our friends. I can still hear them through the vicissitudes of time, your own Robert Mangaliso Sobukwe saying, 'There is only one race in the world, the human race, but the whites have forgotten, and the Arabs have forgotten, and the Chinese have forgotten that it is only us, Africans, who know that there is only one race, the human race. It is our duty to remind them: that is indeed the divine instruction, because the God that I worship cannot be bottled in little religion, the God that I worship cannot be contained in little books. The God that I worship is imminent and omnipresent. He is residence in our minds and in our hearts and in our very veins; it is only we, Africans, who know him in truth.

"We are here this morning not to say new things; we are here to remind ourselves that in the beginning, there was God. And that God created man, and that

man I suspect was an African, and that man could have been nothing else but an African. Why do I suspect so? Because all creation says that man came from the Earth, and as I said, the Earth is either black or brown. So in the beginning there was an African, and in the beginning there was a spirit into which that mould was made alive, and that spirit was God, and I suspect that that God gave us intelligence, and I suspect that that God created Africa where it is in the very middle, because the very middle, the very centre, is the fulcrum, and that is why I suspect Africa it is where it is enjoying not too much cold, enjoying not too much sun: it is in the middle, it is indeed life measured as it should be measured. And that is why I suspect in his divine wisdom he put all the minerals in Africa: if it is not gold, it is coltan, if it is not coltan it is iron-ore, if it is not iron-ore it is copper, and it doesn't stop there.

"When He was distributing rivers and lakes, He ensured that Africa had the best of lakes, the best of rivers, and he did not stop there. He ensured that we are surrounded with the best of the oceans; if it is not the Atlantic it is the Indian, which should be called the African. I do not know why they called it the Indian Ocean. But that is their conspiracy. Then there is the Mediterranean; they also called it another name, and He did not stop there. Once He was done, he ensured that this continent had men and women who are so forgiving, so

generous, that this is the only continent that has welcomed all civilisations."

During a meeting in Brussels, Paul Kagame, the president of Rwanda, was asked about human rights violations and all the corruptions in his country. First of all, it was obvious to me that the journalist wanted to tell her audience that President Kagame had been in power for too long by the way she introduced him as 'President of Rwanda since the year 2000'. The journalist also mentioned that as a combined entity, the European Union is the biggest single contributor to international development with 74 billion euros. What they never tell you in these programmes is how much in total that Europe is sucking out of Africa every year. She then asked him about the human rights in his country Rwanda and this was his response.

"Maybe you need to be looking around in Europe. You are violating people's rights, when we have people being banned and sent back to sink in the Mediterranean and so on. And many people being mistreated in your own countries and so on. Why don't you talk about your own human rights instead of offloading everything?

"You need to stop the superiority complex nonsense about human rights. You think you are the only ones who respect human rights and others violating human rights? No. We fought for human rights and freedom for our people much better, and more than anyone, including

you people who keep talking about this nonsense. Where we have taken our country from to where it is now speaks for itself. The rest of the story has just come from this complex.

He also said to the journalist that she should not be there belittling Africans or leaders of Africa.

On BBC HARDtalk, the interviewer mentioned his critics; President Kagame responded that the critics, *"... have been there from the start, and they don't acknowledge the progress that is being made in the country. It is paralysing in a sense that there are people who have been connected with Rwanda's problems right from the beginning. Even in history for many years they have created these problems. These problems you saw creating genocide and many others are not inherited from Rwanda; they came from outside. So, these are people who have been a part of the problems, and they have always seen Rwanda with a different eye."*

In summary, all they try and do in the Western media is put our leaders down in front of their public. Now the African leaders are beginning to stand up for themselves and tell the truth.

The late Jerry J. Rawlings, 1947-2020, former President of Ghana commented on colonialism, corruption, Western power and democracy. He said, *"We have always believed in and always known the value of democracy long before we were colonised, even after we were colonised. However, the world is going through changes. We have been through the pain of colonialism and today we are going through neo-colonialism, in the sense that, what I'm trying to say is that there was a time when we saw the white men, our colonial powers, as our enemies. Something that is worse than an enemy is a traitor, yes, and when we won our freedom, some of our countries were led by some of the most noble nationalists of our time. But at the same time, with a passage of time, some of them became treacherous and rather betrayed our aspirations. In effect, what I am trying to say is that as bad as an enemy can be, I think something worse than an enemy is a traitor. We have ended up evolving and in the process of trying to modernise, we ended up instead being Westernised, to the point that as I sit here before you, when I wanted to even name my children with African names, heroic names, I am a Catholic, and the Catholic church or something of that character as you know back at home, said no, I cannot, they will have to be Catholic names. I mean, those Catholic names are European names! I went through an argument with this priest, and I said, 'Listen, I have a right to my identity, don't take away my identity, okay?' I mean, Christianise me if you wish, but don't Westernise me.*

"There were times when, my wife and I, she is a graphic artist, we made some beautiful Christmas cards that depicted Christmas in an African setting and the

Christmas cards sold so well, even with white Catholic nuns. We wanted to secure the patent; I went to an office, the registrar general office, to secure the patent. Can you believe that this fellow African, you know, registrar general, looking at my black personality, black face, told me that I could not, this was long after independence, and that it was going to take about three years! I said, 'Why three years?' He said it would have to go to England, and it might take about three years before I'm granted the right to that patent or whatever it is that we register. In other words, in effect what I am trying to say is that, oh, so I have no right to even my creativity? I create my own, you take it away from me and you have to send it to the colonial power? Three years later when they have reproduced it, I have no more right to it. So as an African when you are talking about democracy, etc., let's put it aside.

"Let me bring you to the current modern situation. Since the collapse of the Eastern bloc, we have this unipolar world. The mistakes they are making, you know, by virtue of how they are approaching, especially, let's say, the Iraq and Afghanistan situation, it is undermining international political morality. And what is doing is that it's peculating downwards. So, as it peculates downwards, every mistake you make downward by the time it gets to my country the mistake is multiplied by five times. People in my part of the world are beginning to mimic and take

the cue from the new global leaders.

"What does that mean? Let me give you one fine example. In America, you have Republicans, you have Democrats. You have industries that are strong and independent enough to be able to vote or finance whoever they wish. So, there is certain element of independence, but you come to my country, the new when you are talking about exports, the new situation over the last few years is that those who are in power today in a setting taking the cue from the new global power, Bush's America, the unipolar world, they are destroying every opposition. Any business they think is associated with the opposition has to be destroyed, containing typically of my country. What is happening? National army forces are being denationalised and they are trying to tribalise the army. My dear friend, do you know what you are doing? You are sowing the seed of instability. And yet, and yet, in spite of this, Ghana made a beautiful example in my time, and I'm not taking credit for it, our people did it; all I did was to give our people a leadership of accountability, a leadership of integrity, and our people performed the miracle. And you listening to me? Whether you are from Alaska, I have said it again, Greenland, wherever it is, so long as you give people leadership with integrity, they will always perform the miracle, they will give you the best.

"We did a fantastic job: my time was up, we lost to the opposition. The opposition has been committing the

most atrocious crimes... I'm not saying this because I am in a position; I would have wished that they had continued where we've left off, I would have saluted them and praised them, my country would be flying, but my country is involved in the most massive corruptions, some of the most brutal killings that have taken place, terrorising, you know, recruiting people from their party into the police, the military, etc. And yet, and yet, BBC, CNN, SKY, the American media, the print media are all quiet because they want to portray the image, the image of that fine Ghana as a showcase for the rest of Africa, so they can use Ghana, who has done so well from my time into this time, and they are keeping quiet about the image of this government because they did not want to be undermined... they have enough problems in Afghanistan, they have enough problems wherever it is... so they did not want to lose the situation in Africa in terms of the new world order.

"The unfortunate thing is that I don't care who you (the West) in Italy, in France, in Britain, in America brings into power in my country, but I would wish you would contain them enough from declining into massive corruption and brutality, and tyrant, tyrannical tenancies. Because if you do not contain them, what happens is that they become so corrupt they are now afraid of free and fair election and they refuse to leave power, and then we have volcanic eruptions.

"Sometimes, you know, these superpowers must learn to accommodate, to live and to accept patriotic leadership, patriotic citizens. Too often they (Western powers) are happier with people who are not patriots (bad African leaders). But you in Europe, you never seem to know the roles of some of your bad businessmen. You have good businessmen and I respect them, but some of your bad, bad businessmen are always doing bribes; you know bad things on our continent. And it's our people who suffer."

Kwame Nkrumah, first president of Ghana, Pan-Africanist and one of the founding fathers of the African Union. In part of his speech to his people of Ghana and Africa, said: *"Ghana, your beloved country is free forever. And yet again I want to take the opportunity to thank the chiefs and people of this country, the youths and the farmers, the women, who are so noble, fought and won this battle. Also, I want to thank the brilliant ex-service men who have also co-operated with me on this mighty task of freeing our country from foreign rule and imperialism.*

"I made it quite clear that from now on today we must change our attitude and our minds, we must realise that from now on we are no more a colonial predatory; we are independent people. But also, as I pointed out, that also entails hard work. I am depending upon the millions of the country, the chiefs and people, to help me reshape

the destiny of this country. We are prepared to build it up and make it a nation that would be respected like any other nation in the world. We know we are going to have a difficult beginning, but again, I am relying upon your support, am relying upon your hard work. To see you in these thousands, it doesn't matter how firmer I go, I can see that you are here in your millions.

"And my last warning to you is that you also stand firm behind us, so that we can prove to the world that when the African man is given a chance, he can show to the world that he is somebody. We are above waiting; we shall no longer go back to sleep anymore. We are going to demonstrate to the world, to the other nations, young as we are, that we are prepared to lay our own foundation. As I said in the assembly just a minute ago, I made a point that we are going to see that we create our own African personality and identity. It's the only way in which you can show the world that you are ready for your own battle.

"There is a new Africa in the world. That new African is ready to fight his own battle and show that, after all, the black man is capable of managing his own affairs. But today, I may call upon you all that at this great day, let us all remember that nothing in the world can be done unless it has the purposeful support of God. You have done battle and again; let us rededicate ourselves not only in the struggle to emancipate all the characters in Africa.

Our independence is meaningless unless it is linked up with the total liberation of the African continent."

Malcolm X, speaking on police brutality, democracy, hate and white supremacy in the 1960s said, *"In order for you and me to devise some kind of method or strategy to offset some of the events or repetition of the events that have taken place here in Los Angeles recently, we have to go to the wretch, we have to go to the cause. Dealing with the condition itself is not enough. And it is because of our effort toward getting straight to the root that people often think we are dealing in hate.*

"We are oppressed, we are exploited, we are downtrodden, and we are denied not only civil rights but even human rights. So, the only way we are going to get some of this oppression and exploitation away from us or aside from us is to come together against the common enemy. Who taught you to hate the texture of your hair? Who taught you to hate the colour of your skin to such extent you bleached it to get light like the white men? Who taught you to hate the shape of your nose and the shape of your lips? Who taught you to hate yourself from the top of your head to the soles of your feet? Who taught you to hate your own kind? Who taught you to hate the race you belong to so much so that you don't want to be around each other?

"No... before you come asking Mr Muhammad if he teaches hate, you should ask yourself, who taught you

to hate being what God gave you? I for one as a Muslim believe the white man intelligent enough; if he was made to realise how black people really feel, how fed up we are with that old compromising sweet talk, stop sweet talking, tell him how you feel, tell him what kind of hell you been catching and let him know that if he is not ready to clean his house up he shouldn't have a house that can catch on fire and be burnt down.

"The police are the same way; they put their club upside your head, and then turn around and accuse you of attacking them! Every case of police brutality against the Negro holds the same pattern. They attack you, burst you all upside your mouth and then take you to court and charge you with assault; what kind of democracy is that? What kind of freedom is that? What kind of social or political system is it when a black man has no voice in court, has no nothing on his side other than what the white man choses to give him? My brothers and sisters, we have to put a stop to this, and it will never be stopped until we stop it ourselves. They attacked the victim, and then the criminal who attacked the victim accuses the victim of attacking him! This is American justice, this is American democracy, and those of you who are familiar with it know that democracy in America is hypocrisy. Now if am wrong, put me in jail. But if you can't prove that the democracy is hypocrisy then don't put your hands on me."

James Baldwin debates with William F. Buckley in

1965 at Cambridge University and said that, *"When I was growing up, I was taught in American history books that Africa has no history, and neither did I! That I was a savage, about whom the less said the better, who had been saved by Europe and brought to America. And of course, I believed it; I didn't have much choice. Those where the only books there were. Everyone else seemed to agree; if you walked right out of Harlem, right out of Harlem down town, the world agrees what you see is much bigger, cleaner, whiter, richer, safer than where you are... neglected garbage. People obviously can pay their life insurance, the children look happy, safe, but you are not; then you go back home, and it will seem that, of course, it's an act of God that this is true, that you belong where white people have put you.*

"It is only since the Second World War that there has been a counter image in the world, and that image has not come about due to any legislation in the part or any American government but through the fact that Africa was suddenly on the stage of the world, and Africans had to be dealt with in a way they had never been dealt with before. This gave an American Negro for the first time a sense of a time beyond the savage or a clown. It is created and will create a great many conundrums. One of the great things that the white bro does not know but I think I do know is that black people are just like everybody else, when is used the miss of Negro, and the

miss of colour to pretend and to assume that you are dealing essentially with something exotic, bizarre and practically according to human laws unknown. Alas, that is not true, we are also mercenaries, dictators, murderers, liars; we are human too.

"What is crucial here? It is that unless we can manage to salvage some kind of dialog between those people whom I pretend have paid for the American dream and those other people who have not achieved it, we will be in terrible trouble. I want to say at the end at last, it is that which concerns me most. We are sitting in this room and we would like to think that we are relatively civilised and we can talk to each other on certain levels, so that we could walk out of here assuming that the measure of our enlightenment or at least our politeness has some effect on the world, it may not.

"I remember, for example, when the ex-attorney general Mr Robert Kennedy said that it was conceivable that in 40 years in America, we might have a Negro president. And that sounded like a very emancipated statement, I suppose, to white people. They were not in Harlem, when this statement was first heard, and did not hear and possibly will never hear the laughter and the bitterness in the skull in which the statement was greeted. From the point of view of the man in the Harlem barbershop, Bobby Kennedy only got here yesterday and now he is already on his way to the presidency! We have

been here for 400 years and now he tells us that maybe in 40 years, if you are good, we may let you become president!

"What is dangerous here is a turning away from, the turning away from anything, any white American that says the reason for the political hesitation and spike to the Johnson landslide is one that has been betrayed by American politicians for so long. And I am a grown man and perhaps I can be reasoned with; I certainly hope I can be. But I don't know, and neither does Martin Luther King; none of us know how to deal with those other people whom the white world has for so long ignored who don't believe anything the white world says and don't entirely believe anything I or Martin is saying. And one can't blame them; you watch what is happening to them in less than 20 years."

James Baldwin discussing racism on the Dick Cavett show said, *"I will refer you to an old, old song, no one knows who wrote it, and it was supposed to be spiritual, it was supposed to be about the Christian church, but really, it's a slave, a boat song... the man says, 'If I had my way, if I had my way, little children, great God, if I had my way, I would tear this building down. It is not new for me; we have always felt that it is new for you (the supremacist). And if we were white, if we were Irish, if we were Jewish, if we were pols, if we had in fact in your mind a frame of reference, our heroes would be your heroes, not turning away being here for you instead of turning him into a threat. Malcolm X might still be alive.*

"It is that you can face, in some ways, it is content to white people when they raise their heroes... you know, everyone is proud of brave little Israel. Against them, we don't have nothing. I don't want to be misinterpreted, I'm not an anti-Semite, but you know, when the Israelis pick up guns, or the pols, or the Irish, or any white man in the world, and says, 'Give me liberty or give me death', the entire white world applauds. But when a black man says exactly the same thing, word for word, he is judged a criminal and treated like one, and everything possible is done to make an example of this bad Negro so there won't be any more like him! Now, you can do this if you like... you know, until your party is over. But I know after all who my heroes are, and George Washington is not one of my heroes. For example, neither is Booker T. Washington. What the American public is always trying to do is to accommodate me into system which is always meant my death. They want me to become an accomplice to my own murder; that is what you mean by integration."

Solomon Mahlangu, South African ANC activist and freedom fighter was hanged in 1979, aged 22, for his stance against oppression in his country. His last word before he was killed were, "Tell my people that I love them and they must continue the fight. My blood will nourish the tree that will bear the fruits of freedom. Aluta continua."

Thomas Sankara, former president of Burkina Faso from 1983 to 1987, revolutionist and Pan-Africanist, was assassinated on October 15th, 1987; here he was talking about producing for ourselves, *"Our country produces enough to feed us all; we can even produce more than we need. Unfortunately, for lack of organisation, we still need to beg for food aid. This type of assistance is counterproductive and has kept us thinking that we can only be beggars who need aid. We must put aside this type of aid and succeed in producing more. We must produce, because the one who feeds you usually imposes his will upon you."*

Sankara had this to say about debt and assassination, *"Who in this room does not wish to see our debt simply cancelled? If you don't, you can take the first flight to the World Bank, to go and pay to the World Bank. I would like this conference to clearly declare that we cannot pay the debt, not in a rebellious spirit, but just to avoid assassination individually. In Burkina Faso, I am the only one to refuse and I might not be in the next conference, but on the other hand, with everybody's support and when we are saying that we should not pay the debt, we are not refusing our responsibilities or not keeping our word, it's just that we don't have the same moral standards as others; between the rich and the poor, moral standards cannot be the same.*

"The Bible or the Quran cannot serve those who exploit people, and who exploit those in the same way. We should have two editions of the Bible and two editions of the Quran. Brothers, with everybody's support we will make peace at home; we will be able to use Africa's full potential as well as developing our country because our land is rich. We have enough manpower, and we have a very large market from the North to the South, from the East to the West, we have enough brain power to create or at least to go and learn science and technology where it can be learnt from. Mr President, let's present a united front against a debtor in Addis Ababa. Let's make sure that this conference will decide to limit the arms race between the poor and rich countries. The clubs and knifes that we buy are useless.

"Let's make sure the African market belongs to Africans. Let's produce in Africa, manufacture in Africa, and consume in Africa. Let's produce what we need and consume what we produce instead of exporting goods. Burkina Faso came here to show our locally produced cotton, woven in Burkina Faso, tailored in Burkina Faso, to clothe our own people. I along with my delegation am dressed by our tailors, our farmers; not a single thread comes from Europe or America. I'm not presenting a fashion show here but simply I would like to say that we must accept to live the African way. It's the only way to live in freedom and with dignity. Thank you, Mr President,

our homeland without debt; we will win."

One of the strongest women in the history of Africa is a singer, activist, Pan-Africanist and pioneer of the freedom of Africans. Her name is Miriam Makeba. Makeba's voice was spiritual, motivating and empowering to all Africans. Her smile was as bright as the brightest sunshine of Africa, shining through each note she sang. The Apartheid in South Africa saw her influence as a threat and decided to exile her from her own country where she was born and raised. The Western tribes that arrived did this because she was a voice for her people. The same old saying, 'You cut the head off the snake, the body is powerless'; this was how Africa and her people were treated, and this is how we are still being treated but in a more advanced and silenced way.

Here are some of our beautiful queens' talking on racism, transgression, imperialism and brutality; this was an interview produced in 1969.

Interviewer: "Mrs Makeba, are people happy in Johannesburg?"

MM: "That depends on which people you are talking about. When we speak of people in Johannesburg, we have to be specific in that in South Africa there are two separate communities, and that's the white community and the black community. Ah… I will speak for my community. I think we are happy, we dance, we sing, because to us, sometimes it's better to laugh to keep from crying."

Interviewer: "What is the message you want to give, to transmit to the public, to your listeners?"

MM: "I always feel that, even though one is an artist, we are first human beings and we live in the same world as any other person, so that we as artists should never close our eyes to what is happening around us. Therefore, coming from South Africa, naturally my life was affected by my environment there, and the songs that I sing are just about my everyday life. And, ah… the things that I say are those that have affected my life. The message I am trying to give to my audience is not one, I am just trying to make them understand me as a person and my country and my people."

Interviewer: "Do you see some principal differences between the struggles of Africans in countries like South Africa, Mozambique, Angola, on one hand, and on the other hand in countries like Brazil and the United States where they are in a minority?"

MM: "There is really no difference in the struggles between the people you have mentioned because we are all Africans, we were just put in different countries by white people who took the people from Africa and spread them out. And it is true that our problems are the same. Now, saying that they are a minority, this really means nothing because the white man, wherever he is, whether he is in the majority or the minority, he rules! It just proves to everyone that we just have to keep fighting, we just have to fight that much more because it doesn't matter whether he is a majority or minority, he is always on top."

Interviewer: "Which status are you aiming to between the white and the Africans at the end when you have won?"

MM: "That will depend on them. We are not worried about them; we are just worried about ourselves. It is our country; they came from Europe to invade our country, they took it, they have made us suffer. So we don't have to worry about thinking what we will do to them, what will happen to them. It will be up to them to see fit what they can do when we have won, just like they see fit what to do right now while they are on top. So it is something that we don't worry about. All we are worried about is to fight and liberate ourselves. What will happen after that will depend again on the invaders. They could have come to our country and lived side by side with us, we didn't mind that; in fact, when they came, we said, 'Come in, sit down', and when they sat down, they said, 'Get out', and now it will be up to them.

"It is known that Africa only had black people, Europe had white people, Asia had yellow people; now it is absurd to say that we Africans were not in Africa when white people first came! And secondly, the conquerors write history; they came, they conquered, and they wrote.

Now, you don't expect people who came to invade us to write the truth about us? They will always write negative things about us, and they have to do that because they have to justify their invasion in all the countries. It's like saying when the Europeans went to America there were no Indians there! It's ridiculous because they were there. I know that my people were there. We don't write our history; it has always been handed down to us orally by our elders. Of course, the white man came and he wrote history. In fact, you don't know anything about any place until the white man gets there. Like my husband always said, 'It's like saying, well, until the white man comes to any place, nothing lives; it's only when he comes, he says, boom! I have discovered you, now you exist!' Which is ridiculous. And that is why I had to say the things I say in my performances because I know again that I am right, and because I am right, I know I will win, because the truth shall never be covered by lies.

"I have difficulties in many different places, and not only me... ah, if you are black, you have difficulties everywhere there are white people. And most white people say that we should not generalise and so on and so forth. And in fact, there are some countries even, take Sweden; in Sweden people say there are no racial problems there, but it is only because there are not that many black people in Sweden, so you don't really see it as clearly as you see it in countries like the United States or even South

Africa. But there is prejudice everywhere; for instance, in Sweden, we were performing there and my guitarist who isn't really white, he is a Brazilian, he looks white because he is an albino. But some people approached him on four occasions and asked him why does he have to play with Niggas? And this was in Sweden where people very often say they have no (racial) problems.

"And take his country, Brazil; we were there last June and white people in Brazil denied the fact that there was racial problem in Brazil. But it exists; we saw it every day. Everywhere I performed in Brazil, I never saw black people, I only performed to white people! And they said, 'Well, it's because they can't afford to come here, it's too expensive', which is another form, I mean, that is another form of keeping them from where they can enjoy themselves together with white people, they keep them poor, so that we have problems everywhere. Sometimes people send us threatening letters and some send very vile letters and tell us Niggas get out of here and go. So, there is no way to run, eh, we just have to stay wherever we are and fight to liberate ourselves."

A 1988 interview quoted in her book: *"I look at an ant and I see myself, a native South African endowed by nature with a strength much greater than my size, so I might cope with the weight of a racism that crushes my spirit. I look at a bird and I see myself, a native South African soaring above the injustices of Apartheid on wings of pride, the pride of a beautiful people. I look at a stream and I see myself, a native South African flowing irresistibly over the obstacles until they become smooth and one day disappear, flowing from the origin that has been forgotten towards an end that will never be.*

MM on exile: "I think that when you are in exile, you are in exile... whether famous or not, exile is painful!"

MM talking about Sangoma (traditional healers): "I know that it's very difficult for Westerners to believe because when a people become colonised, the first thing they do is to strip you of your own culture and impose that of their own to be able to manipulate you much better."

MM talking about language and traitors: "We were not allowed to sing in English; we didn't care because we sang in our own languages and there were songs we sang that were very detrimental to them. They didn't understand until some of us, because in every revolution in every country you will always find someone within the oppressed to collaborate with the oppressor, some people went and told them. Watch these people because they are arousing the consciousness of the people in that they are singing this and that song, which means this and that, and then those songs were banned."

After 28 years since she was exiled and her songs were allowed to be played again, she was asked what she felt and if it made her exile easier or harder. This was her response: *"It makes me happy in that all these years they have tried to separate me from my home and from the people at home. It seems as though the people at home have never forgotten me, as well as I have never forgotten them, which means that blood is thicker than mud and there is nothing that can come between us. I'm also happy that the people at home have decided that they are not going to sit down and take Apartheid just lying down. They said no, which is why there is such interest today in South Africa. It doesn't come from me, from anyone out here; it comes from the people from within, and I am saying, 'Thank you to my people', because that means that we will get there and I shall go home."*

Her case resembles many of our freedom fighters, how they were punished for taking a stance on their rights and freedom for their people. Today, if we put down every case of what the Western world did to our people, it would fill a library of books. What is so sad and so cruel today is when people cannot see these facts and instead try to reason with us, the bashing we have taken from those we have allowed to come, sit and have dinner with us is difficult to fathom. Worst of all is when we take a stand, we are looked upon as inciting hate and violence. It is a very sad world, and we as people have a duty to try and put things together and make this world a better place.

A strong African with a strong voice who can educate and give our people a sense of pride and direction will be under the watchful eyes of the evil ones that are in the dark. Their role is to assassinate you and if they do not, they will strive to break your spirit and turn your people against you. They will hurt you until you are almost at your last breath and you have not got the strength to continue, then like a pack of vultures they will eat you.

This is why I believe that all the laws and rules formed under the name of democracy by the Western world do nothing but protect their own image and shield them from the atrocities they have committed around the world. There is a serious fear by the Western government that one day there will be some sort of retaliation by the new generation, whose ancestors were punished and brutalised by the imperialist states. Clearly, there is a monumental effort to keep Africa as far backward and corrupt as possible because of those fears.

The whole world is played in two scenes. The one you see in the media and books, which usually are not the truth and only serve as distractions. The other one you do not see, which is the truth that is carefully kept secret in the dark. If the ordinary citizens who have empathy for humanity know what is in the dark and what their leaders are doing to others, they would be emboldened to rebel against the perpetrators of crimes against humanity.

Dr Arikana Chihombori Quao, former AU ambassador, Pan-Africanist and activist, addressed the African diaspora in the US in 2019. She begins: *"Good evening, African diaspora... The more I begin to understand, not only our*

Africa, but the more I begin to understand us as black people, why is it that we are the most disrespected on Earth? No matter where you find us on this globe. They often wonder why these black people are so smart and so indestructible. Maybe it's because of that third eye...! No, it is the melanin, that's what makes us special. That's what makes us the origin of humanity, which is our motherland, our motherland Africa. The continent with everything and anything the world needs, the continent that everybody is going to for their needs, but the continent that we the children of Africa are busy running away from. That keeps me up every night. The more I try to dig deeper in understanding why Africa is where Africa is today, I can't help but find myself repeatedly going back to the beginning, to say, 'How did we end up where we are, as Africans, how did we get here?' Not only as black people but as Africans.

"The colonisers started coming to Africa, starting with the Portuguese, followed with slavery. But by 1884 after they had been haphazardly going to our continent, looting from the Africans, pretty soon they started looting from each other the loot that they looted from the Africans, and before you know it, they were killing each other, and they were ready to have a European war on the African soil. So, Bismarck, the chancellor of Germany at that time, called his sidekick, King Leopold of Belgium, and said, 'Listen, we've got a problem; we are getting ready

to kill each other in a heavy European war in African. Why don't you call all the colonisers – France, Germany, Italy, Spain, Portugal, Belgium, and of course mighty Britain? Let's all meet in Berlin, Germany, and strategise on how we can organise ourselves so we can effectively see to it that Africa and her children are defeated and dominated.'

"They considered breaking up our Africa into tiny little countries that we know of today. Our economies are designed to see that they will never make it on their own, and even if those small economies do make it, they are easy to destabilise. Who in their right mind put a country together like the Gambia, Burundi, Togo, Djibouti, Lesotho, Swaziland (now Eswatini) and many, if not all, African countries? Each one of them was given the same sovereignty as China. If the world was to be a boxing game, you see in boxing they understand that heavyweight belongs to a heavyweight boxing ring, middleweights are in the middleweight, and lightweights and wannabes want to be in their ring. You don't take a wannabe boxer and throw them in the same ring with heavyweights.

"But what's been done to our Africa, let's start negotiating with each country against country. Countries, please stand up. Little Gambia, stand up, and Gambia was supposed to negotiate with China! Lesotho is supposed to negotiate with India, Swaziland must jump in with

the United States, and Djibouti, you must go in. You see, the Europeans realised as individual European countries, they can't make it, so they came together as the European Union so then they negotiate as a block, so here Djibouti – you go in with the EU. And when the African countries lose, the world stands back and says, 'Hey, what's wrong with your African countries? Why aren't you able to manage your people? How can that be? Where is the parity?' African countries are like wannabe boxers who are constantly thrown into the heavyweight boxing ring, and we are getting our rear ends kicked day in and day out.

"1884, fast forward to 2019, nothing has changed. The strategy that was put in place to see to it that Africa and her children are forever defeated and dominated remains alive and well. And yet in our minds we tend to think that the Berlin conference is a thing of the past! Well, my brothers and sisters, the Berlin conference is alive and well. And allow me to take it home for you! Have you even wondered why inter-African trade is sitting at 18%? I will tell you why. We have 43 different currencies on the continent. It is difficult to trade with each other because of the currencies. It is easier for us to exchange with the US dollars, with the euros, than with each other. Why is that? The Berlin conference! It's easier for Mozambican to sell Mozambican oil outside Mozambique, to Europe and everywhere else, just so Zimbabwe next door can

buy it from across the oceans. It's easier for a company that is manufacturing the best ceramic tiles in Africa, in Egypt, that company's sends its tiles to Italy only for the Africans to turn around and buy the same tiles, twenty, thirty times the cost. Why is it that we are not trading with each other? Because, starting in South Africa, there is a road that goes up until maybe two three kilometres from the border with Botswana, and that same road picks up two three kilometres into Botswana; if only we could connect the two, but the Berlin conference says no, you are different, you are another country.

"You can look at it this way: if we were to connect all the existing powerlines in Africa today, we would provide electricity to 30 million more people, and in the process, we would save 20 billion dollars. But what is the reason we can't connect the powerlines? Thanks to the Berlin conference. We are different countries. We can't cross that border. Why are our children crossing the Mediterranean in search of nothing? It is because little Gambia could create so many jobs. And the young men in Gambia, Gambia which is surrounded by Senegal, cannot go to Senegal and look for a job thanks to the Berlin conference.

"The question then becomes, if you look at all the issues we are dealing with today in Africa one by one, every one of them relates to the Berlin conference and our inability to work together as one continent, one Africa,

speaking with one voice, thanks to the Berlin conference."

Ama Ata Aidoo, nee Christina Ama Aidoo, activist, author, poet, and playwright when she was interviewed in 1987 about Europe's involvement in Africa, this was her response: *"The thing is that as far as I'm concerned, since we met you people (Europeans) five hundred years ago, 'Look at us. We've giving everything, you are still taking'. It's true, I mean, where would the whole Western world be without Africa? Our cocoa, our timber, our gold, our diamonds, our platinum, our whatever... everything you are is us. I am not just saying it, it's a fact. And in return for all of this, what have we (Africans) got? Nothing.*

"Anti-personality indoctrination against ourselves; if you go and cook up your horrible diseases like aids, you say it is us, you brought us tuberculosis, we didn't have this big cough until white people came here, in exchange for Africa giving Europe five hundred solid years of our people – I mean, not Europe, the Western world – of our human beings to work your canes, to dig your gold, to take gold itself, diamonds, I mean, you know... fish, peanuts, palm oil everything, in exchange for that... we have got nothing, nothing, and you know it. Nothing. And white folks look upon us like monkeys! It is true; it's in your literature. You know, some of your best thinkers have said this about us. Have you heard about all this Germans? Have you heard? They said, Lord Burton, people like that, they said we don't even have the

brains of animals – that's what we got from you people.

Interviewer: "But don't you think that this is over now?"

Aidoo: "Over where? Is it over? Who said that aids came from the green monkey? Is it over? Is it over...?"

Interviewer: "Well, if this is your impression, do you think you can ever forgive us?"

Aidoo: "It's not a question of forgiveness. I have nothing against you. My point is that you did and you are doing it for your survival, what is necessary. We can't blame you for that. The fact that we didn't do enough for our own survival, and we are still not doing enough for our survival, that is not your problem. You know, everybody that God has created has a sense of survival, you know, and until... if we don't develop it, we can't blame white people. You came here because you needed these things; you took gun powder from the Chinese and you needed them to shoot people."

Interviewer: "Do you consider aid as a new form of colonisation?"

Aidoo: "Of course. You know, my people, the Akans, we have a proverb, it says that 'good morning, thank you' is never enough to sort anybody's food forever, and you cannot build your life on thank you, thank you, thank you, morning, thank you, English, thank you, you know? Which is what aid makes; we are always receiving, receiving. Nobody looks, and I don't care who he is, nobody anywhere in this world is going to send you their best of anything. Do you see? Neither the expert nor... what I mean, people, you give us what you can afford; aid is the leftovers really and it cannot be enough... what I mean, now the world is one place, so, there is nothing wrong if my house is in a crisis and you offered me something... there is nothing wrong, you know, because there is an inter-relationship, but a whole nation (Ghana), a whole continent (Africa), cannot live forever on aid. And I think aid is... we are, in Africa, we are in danger of making foreign aid a kind of policy... that is wrong, I mean, I think that it humiliates our people. The people in the villages have not asked anybody to go round begging on their behalf."

Ama Ata Aidoo on writing and unfairness in business: *"Well, being a writer, really, it is crazy; I mean it is a very self-consuming kind of activity. You know, you sit in a room ba, ba, ba... you write, and you think that other people outside want to hear it. Writing a book is tense; when you finish writing the book you are tense because you wonder, ah, how would the publishers and editors react to a book, to a story? Ah... even when it is published you wonder, why are they saying my books are selling in Ghana, in Nigeria, in Sierra Leone, Botswana, Lesotho, even South Africa, ah, Kenya, and I'm still so poor?! So, all these issues are part of the horror of being a woman, a writer and African! But you don't stop writing because of any of them, you just go on."*

One Special Story of a Fallen African Giant and a Great Nation

Every coup and assassination by our strong and rightful leaders are carefully planned and organised behind closed doors, by the same old imperialist states and organisations that claim to have colonised Africa and her people around the world. The physical work is always done by someone of the same race so that it looks like black-on-black crime. This is nothing but another negative attitude towards African people, because every race, society, and community cause more crime against their own people on a national scale but only black crimes are singled out by many. This is just bizarre to me.

The murders, the hate, the plots and plans are all done secretly by those whose ambitions are power and money. I call them the 'world secret killing machines', and these are include the FBI, CIA, MI5 and MI6, the Belgian QUAERO ET TEGO and the French Direction Generale de la Securite Exterieure (DGSE).

Let us once more look at one of our heroes who suffered at the hands of colonial imperialists.

Patrice Lumumba. He was a young and brilliant man who had a vision for his people and his country of the Democratic Republic of Congo (DRC). He was a visionary. As a free thinker who could not play the puppet for the imperialist government, he led his country to independence and became the first democratic elected prime minister of his nation. He gave his time and put his own life in danger for what he believed in as a citizen of the DRC; that the Belgian oppressors were only interested in reaping the wealth of the country whilst enslaving and disrespecting the people. A bright young man seeking justice for his people was now seen as a threat to the Western governments that were involved in the DRC. Covertly, his assassination was planned by the Belgian authorities, the CIA and the US government and other allies, including MI6, as I discovered when I searched deeper.

Patrice was portrayed as a communist and a dictator by the very same imperialists because he was not appeasing their interests. His only intention was to build his nation and help his people live with freedom, respect and equality within their own country. However, he was cast as Satan even though he harmed no one, not even the Western people who took over his country. Those who robbed, tortured, and killed the people of Congo are now seen on world media, in schools and in museums as our saviours.

Here are some of the testimonies of those who were involved or were eyewitnesses and researchers into his assassination in 1961. I watched a documentary presented by Michel Noll and titled 'Death Colonial Style: The

Execution of Patrice Lumumba'.

Gerard Soete was a former Katanga police officer who said he kept one of Lumumba's teeth as a souvenir because he knew Lumumba was a very important public and political figure.

The man who knows why and how Patrice was killed was a Belgian colonial official and diplomat, Jacques Brassine. He said Patrice was a danger to the Western people in the sense that he was not open to the kind of solution that their countries wanted to apply.

Louis Marliere was a colonel in the Belgian secret service that also played a big part in the fall of Patrice Lumumba. He said Lumumba chose the wrong side. Louis naively believed that Patrice was a communist and chose Russia and the Soviets over the Western world.

Virginia, USA, was where CIA agent Larry Devlin lived. He also said that Lumumba was a danger for both the Congo and the rest of the world. So, Larry was the man the US trusted to carry out the assassination of Lumumba. He continued to say that Patrice allowed the Soviets to come in and the US government believed that the Soviets would take over the Congo.

Juliana Lumumba was Patrice's daughter and minister of culture; she believed that her father was a symbol of nationalism and struggle for independence, and that he sacrificed himself to pursue those ideals till the end. After her father's assassination, it was forbidden to talk about his death, but now the people of Congo need to know more about him because it is the history of the Congolese people. There is a great desire for the people to know about the founding fathers of their independence, and yet the people of Congo and Africa still do not know enough.

Kinshasa was called Leopoldville. Lumumba was the first black prime minister of the DRC. In his words, he said the people/masses of the Congo needed bread and progress, and they needed to be able to build their nation.

Roland Lumumba, Patrice's son, was less than three years old when he last saw his dad. Both he and the people of Congo want to know why his father was killed. It is their duty now to pass on the truth to the younger generation and beyond.

Jean Van Lierde, a friend of Lumumba said he, Patrice, was a free man and that people found him so original as a black man who did not lick the feet of the colonialists. They instinctively targeted him as a threat to the West. It was that freedom of his which turned him into this kind of meteoroid that flashes bright across the skies and then disappears.

The first Europeans to arrive in the Congo described it as the heart of darkness. In 1955, when King Boudewijn visited the country, the colonial order still seemed secure, but millions of Congolese paid with their lives during the 80 years of Belgian rule.

Lumumba was a local post office worker who became

the leader of an unstoppable independent movement for the Congo. Patrice Lumumba said the objective that they were pursuing was the liberation of the Congo from colonial control and the total emancipation of the country. He also said, "We certainly know exactly where we are going. The independence of Congo doesn't mean driving the Belgians out or breaking with Belgium. It's quite the opposite, we want to form a sovereign government which will provide a place for everyone, where Congolese and Belgians will be able to work hand in hand in the service of the Congolese nation."

I cannot imagine the Belgian government or politicians would say the same thing in reverse about Congo! If the Congolese brutally took over Belgium, could you really imagine that they would then accept a dual form of sovereign government and work hand in hand. This is how kind we Africans are! We accept everyone and forgive everyone even though they brutalised us to the lowest possible status.

Patrice won the first free election and became the first prime minister of the country through the MNC party, and Belgium reluctantly handed the government to him.

Patrice's first clash came at the independence celebration in 1960. King Boudewijn's speech sounds to me like the same old mastermind game they had played in Africa and around the world through the media. Imperialists always act in front of the press, cameras and people that they are saviours and angels, but that is not the case. Here was the Belgian King flaunting his power and boasting about what his country had allegedly done for the Congo: "Gentlemen, the independence of the Congo is a crowning moment of the mission conceived by the genius of King Leopold II undertaken by him with a courageous tenacity and pursued with great perseverance by Belgium."

The Belgians thought the speech of their king was great, in which he exalted the role of Belgium talking about everything they had brought to the Congo. He continued by saying that they arrived at the moment when Belgium had decided to grant the Congo its independence, which was all well and good; a classic speech for that moment. Then Joseph Kasa Vubu, the first president, made a speech thanking the king and talking about the future of the Congo. Kasa Vubu's speech was applauded because he said what the Belgians want to hear; he was the kind of president that the colonial oppressors wanted in office. He was the masters' puppet.

Patrice Lumumba was not scheduled to speak. I can see in the footage that he was furious that everyone was bowing to the same people that had tortured, looted and killed millions for no other reason than the natural resources of the Congo. These so-called men and saviours are respected and hailed as heroes even by those who should stand and fight for their people. Patrice was an angel sent by God to be there for those who did not have a voice. Belgium had the audacity to come to a wealthier country, 76 times bigger than itself, cause atrocities, and yet our people granted them respect!

I can see why Patrice Lumumba took the initiative to put things in their rightful place. His speech came as a shock because no one was expecting it, it shocked the Belgian authorities who already knew how powerful Lumumba was. The Belgians knew if Lumumba was given the chance to speak, he would tell the truth. The Belgians did not want this to be seen or heard on live TV and by the media. Lumumba was left out of the guest list of speakers. The Belgian authorities were acting again as the holy saviours of the Congo. The people knew that they were not as such, but I guess the devil always comes in the form of an angel.

Kasa Vubu was not a truth teller, the Belgians knew that, this is why he was their choice. He was not a threat to their interests in the Congo even if they granted the Congolese so-called independence. He was more like the humble servant of his cruel master.

The Belgians believe that Lumumba condemned the colonisation of his country because he reported the harsh treatments by the colonial oppressors. For example, the Belgian authorities were cutting off the limbs and enslaving citizens of the Congo. He pointed out that the Belgians had killed millions of his people and that nothing was in place for the benefit and interest of the people of Congo. The Belgians and their allies knew Lumumba was the real deal with the potential to get his people out of this mess. He was the head of the snake and he had the power to influence the nation. They wanted to appear to listen and support his ideas. In truth, the Belgians knew they must put a stop to his righteous effort to make Congo a great nation and to make the world aware of their dark deeds.

Because of his genuine care for his people and his country, the Belgians and their allies did not want the world to know the truth, they made Lumumba the bad guy, an evil person, a threat to his people and the world.

So here is the surprise speech of Lumumba: *"You who have fought for independence and are today victorious, I salute you in the name of the Congolese government, I salute all my friends who fought relentlessly at our side. We have been subjected to insult, sarcasms, to the blows we have had to endure from morning to night just because we were Africans. We learnt that the law was never the same according to when it was applying to white or black. Who will forget the shooting of the barbarous jail cells waiting those who refuse to submit to the regime of injustice, oppression and exploitation?"*

The Congolese people clapped and gave him a standing ovation. This provoked and revealed the darkness of the oppressor's act in the Congo; they did not even have the decency to apologise to the Congolese people, but instead got angry with Lumumba. Van Lierde, Lumumba's friend, thought that when he made that famous speech, that was the precise moment when he signed his death warrant. The Belgian government did not want him because he did not fit in with them, the Americans or other businesspeople and their interests.

Rene Smal, of the Belgian secret service, believes that if it was not for the small Belgian army suppressing the Congolese army, things would have been terrible. Five days after the new state was formed and the speech of Lumumba, a riot broke out between the Congolese army and the Belgian army. What we know now is that the Belgian government sent paratroopers into the Congo to help their people and to secure their interests. In the rich cooper province of Katanga (which was controlled by the Belgian government), Lumumba's opponent Moise Kapend Tshombe called for help from the Belgian government to disarm the black troops. Ten days later after gaining independence on the June 30th, 1960, the colonial soldiers triumphantly returned to the former colony. Jacques Bartelous, former chief aide to Tshombe said that in less than 24 hours, it was all over thanks to the Belgians.

Jean Baptiste Kibwe, former finance minister, said: "The rebellion started on the 9th and lasted till the 10th of July, and on the 11th of July, 5PM, they declared independence (for Katanga). Tshombe, known as Mr. Cash Register, declared himself as the president of a separate province, but he was a president installed by the Belgians."

Rene Smal said: "*Elisabethville was above all a centre for important financial interest that was where the Union Minier, the mining company was, obviously, Belgium financial companies wanted to keep their hands on that. One of the major figures in the breakaway state was Minister of Finance Jean Baptiste Kibwe: as soon as we took over the mining company Union Minier, he continued to export and the revenue from this went into the Katanga bank.*" Tshombe's principal aide was a Belgian chief lawyer named Jacques Bartelous. He said that the mining companies now paid their taxes and license fees to the Katanga government, not to the Leopoldville.

The Belgian authorities had seized the Congo and our people and had set up back door corruptions and inhumane treatments. Despite the torture and brutal murder of our people, they had the nerve to tell the world that they seek democracy when they still believe that they helped the Congo! There is too much corruption in the country. It baffles me why Belgium is not paying for what they stole from our people. They manipulated the system and set up their own illegal government by using the Congolese people, who were ambitious for power to turn against Lumumba. Before they showed up in the Congo, the people were living just fine without the hate and corruption which the Belgians and their allies brought to the people of Africa.

I still do not understand why most people's first impression of Africa is corruption; this is what they have been fed through education, media and literature. Even people who have been to Africa and have seen the level of poverty and corruption do not seem to be able to come to terms with why Africa looks the way it does. Hundreds of years of manipulation and Western colonisation is still affecting the people of Africa, and it is hard to make an immediate change.

When I point out these things to most people, they will say to me, "Hey, Sam, but your people are now independent and in control!"

Well, yes, that is the way it appears now, but behind closed doors it is not the same.

The African people for thousands of years have lived among each other without conflict, hate or tribalism. There is no evidence to show that we were barbaric towards each other until the continent was invaded. Corruption was taught to the African people by the oppressors; if you can keep people occupied by hating and fighting each other, then you can exploit them. This is what has been done for hundreds of years and still continues today. We are paying the price for allowing the oppressors to continue their secret corruptive behaviour. Corruption is one of the worst viruses introduced to our system and the minds of African people. It has been ingrained in us for so long that many of our people will trust and accept their colonial counterparts on any level of decision making, education, religion or law making. Our religion and education do not reflect the true history and culture of Africa and our people. We embraced everything that was given to us even though it does not improve our lives.

This is like holding on to a hot iron that is burning your hand, but you just cannot let go; you want to please those who teach you to hate yourself and your people. You show empathy, respect, and forgiveness towards them despite all the human, political and economic atrocities they have caused for Africans throughout the world.

In a documentary, Bartelous says that the tax money paid to the Katanga government enabled them to equip the Katangan army (Jondans) and buy weapons and armoured vehicles. He continues to say there were arms merchandisers that continued to visit Tshombe's home to try and sell him weapons. This is a win-win for the oppressors because they are now selling arms to the people, letting them fight and kill each other while harvesting their resources free of charge. They deliberately support corrupt people with guns and money to control them like puppets while the local people are left to suffer. These very same oppressors are portraying themselves as saviours and aid providers through the media, convincing people that they bring Western democracy to the innocent, when this is not the case at all.

This is a game which they have played for centuries. It is like a teacup that looks clean from the outside, but inside it is as dark as anything can be. They played the good part of a saint in front of the world media, yet those that are the real saints are portrayed as the devil. The media, education systems, movies, museums and libraries are all part of this global manipulation. Therefore, today we still believe in the oppressors' religions and ways of doing things because we have been led to believe that we were the bad ones.

The plans, wars and coups are all done behind closed doors and the strings are pulled by the colonisers. They do not care how many people suffer from the terror they created and the violent treatments they used against African people.

Tshombe, the Belgians' choice, had a white mercenary army that was there to protect him and his puppet masters. They claimed to be defending the free will in the heart of Africa, which soon became known as 'les Afro' – literally 'the dreadful men'. There was anger by the Congolese people in Leopoldville for the breakaway country. This was the reaction that the oppressors wanted. Less than a quarter of the people in the Congo had seen their own resources, yet it caused so much uncertainty for them that I am sure the poor people were wishing that their homeland was never so blessed with such a wealth of resources that seems to be attracting evil people.

Lumumba said that the plot was already prepared, and they intended to oppose a government against the wishes of the people of Congo. In my opinion, he was referring to the Belgian government and their allies. He had already seen what was coming from the two faces of the Belgian government and those who were working in hand with the Belgium authority. Lumumba continues; "Belgium wants to balkanize this country to break up the Congo."

Larry Devlin, CIA, said that Lumumba asked for US troops to come and replace the Belgian soldiers. They talked to the US ambassador 'Kimberlake', who realised that if the US troops did go, almost immediately Russian troops would follow. The ambassador asked them to send in UN troops instead of the Americans to resolve the situation.

As requested, the UN decided to replace the Belgian troops with UN forces. The US believed this would stop the Soviets making propaganda of the US from the Congo crisis. But US planes were re-sprayed and flew into the Congo as UN planes. Lumumba called for the UN troops to help end the conflict that was unfolding, but when the UN arrived, they took no action against Tshombe and the separatists.

General Rikhye, Indian former military adviser to the

UN, said Mr. Lumumba and the other leaders had the wrong idea of how to use the UN. He explained that they expected the UN to behave like a big power providing arms, equipment and intelligence. As the people of Congo celebrated the arrival of the UN, the Soviet prime minister Nikita Khrushchev was holding talks concerning the prospect of the Red Army for the Lumumba government.

Without any official invitation, Lumumba travelled to the US to ask for support against the Belgian intervention. But the 'jungle premier', as Lumumba was called, was not even received by the US president, Dwight D Eisenhower. As you can see, everyone was fighting for their own interests. They cared nothing for the lives of the Congolese people, so long as they got what they wanted.

In his speech in the US, Lumumba said: "I wish to convey to the American people a message of friendship from the people of Congo. We have great faith in you, we want you to understand and help us. We want you to know that when your technicians and teachers come to our country, they will find in the Congolese people friends and brothers."

CIA agent Larry Devlin said: "African leaders were new to us; a man such as Patrice Lumumba didn't have sophistication or the power, if you like, like the Germans, French, English, and what have you, diplomat? And he tends to say things very bluntly, which upsets the West."

If Larry Devlin's statement was not blunt, then I do

not know what bluntness is. In their mind, for us to deal with the West we have to be able to act and speak the way they want. Well, Larry and many others must realise that this world is a very big place and many countries around the world do not speak or do things like the US. He said our leaders do not have the sophistication of big European imperialist countries. His take on Lumumba and the African leaders just show how much they disrespect us and our people. This kind of statement just serves as a guide as to how we are looked at by the leaders and authorities of the Western world.

The US and the UN could not help Lumumba. They knew that rejecting him would mean he had to submit himself or make irrational decisions that would lead him to the traps that were being set for him by the oppressors and their close allies. So, what did Lumumba do? He turned to the Soviets for help. This served as proof for the American government and the Belgians accuse him of being the enemy. Dirty politics at its best. They will not help the Congolese people, yet they will take their resources and make bombs to kill others, then reject their safety.

In film footage, Belgian Louis Marliere says that they put a listening device in Lumumba's office. He admits that it was the Americans who provided the equipment. He continues by saying they intercepted all of Lumumba's conversations and got a translator, as he was speaking his native language. So, they already knew what he was saying and what he intended to do. Why they were plotting to kill a man who was the head of a nation that is so great in Africa is something that may, for some, be hard to understand. Why do these people have the right to do all these evil acts while lying about it as they torture and kill the strong leaders of our continent?

This is why I get frustrated when people around the world express to me that Africans are very corrupt. If the truth was told about what the whole world has done to us, and people finally held their nations responsible, then this world would be a better place. But as I know too well, we have a long way to go.

Lumumba exposed the foreign intervention which attempted to undermine the new independence of Congo. The press transmits what they are paid to by those who control the narrative. They started to brand Lumumba as a threat to the world interest.

The style of a report from a German correspondent was typical of those used in the Western media. The report described his eyes as 'rolling through his glasses, there is something terrible about [him]'. The creation of negative propaganda around his image had started to spread so that the world would view Lumumba as a devil.

This type of mass media propaganda is still being used today. If you control the TV, radio and newspapers, you have at your disposal some of the best ways to tarnish someone's character. Because of the way people are educated in the Western world, we cannot blame the ordinary citizens for their lack of understanding about Africa, as they genuinely trust that their government tell the truth. I must say, there are some people who know the truth, but they just do not care because it is not their race or people who are suffering. There are those who do not care about us because we are seen as lesser human beings compared to them. But I must also admit that people in today's world should not listen to governments, schools or institutions that tell you how to love, hate or feel about other people. Our responsibility is to make sure we use our common sense and put ourselves in others' shoes and see what it would be like if you experienced the same treatment meted out to them.

It is ironic that our leaders in Africa are classed as the most corrupt by the very same people who are pulling the strings in the dark. This is like a manipulated photograph; you see the beautiful image, but you do not see those that are working hard behind the camera and on Photoshop. Without them, the picture they want you to see would not exist. Most of the corruption, wars and coups in Africa would not exist today if those behind the curtain stopped pulling the strings and glorifying themselves as leaders of a free world and democracy.

Lumumba's daughter, Juliana Lumumba, was with her father in most of the press conferences. She said in the Belgium press that her father was portrayed as Satan with the devil's horns and was likened to a communist. She said her dad was only saying things that were in the minds of the Congolese people, but these were not part of the mindset and objectives of the colonial oppressors at the time.

Lumumba wanted first and foremost for the Congolese people to be worthy of their culture. He said, "We want to be independent but with quality and respect." I ask again, what more can a nation do when their wealth is enriching others, yet their own people are treated like worthless animals? I would have liked to have asked someone like Larry Devlin, if he were still alive today, to answer this question, if he would have accepted these types of treatments in his own backyard?

When Lumumba was asked by the press, "Are you a communist?", he replied, "You always make me laugh when I am asked this question." He smiled. "I'm not a communist at all… you know, I have often been presented as a communist, anti-white and anti-Belgian, and someone destructive! I'm absolutely not, I am simply a nationalist leader and I'm not a communist and will never be."

Larry Devlin admitted that he received $100,000 from the CIA with the instruction to make the elimination of Lumumba the priority goal of his mission. In the documentary, Larry continues by saying, "Yes, I received the cable that someone whom I would… a senior officer

I would know by sight… would arrive and give me a specific instruction. I was surprised." In a Belgian secret service telegraph, there were talks of a mysterious operation called 'Barracuda'. Louis Marliere recalls; "They sent two people to talk to me about the Lumumba affair who were in favour of eliminating him."

Larry Devlin: "I remember being totally surprised when Louis Marliere instructed me that they wanted to get rid of him. I never heard such a thing, that an agent was involved in such things before."

Louis Marliere: "They wanted to send me a 'crocodile killer' to get rid of Lumumba, that's what they came to propose."

Larry Devlin: "Substances used to eliminate Lumumba were toothpaste with poison, which will result in an illness similar to polio, something like that, I remember."

Louis Marliere: "I never opposed it; I let them get on with it. I think there were lots of people who prefer to get PL out of their way (the Western government and business entities)."

Devlin believed at that time it was a US presidential order to eliminate Patrice Lumumba.

Again, if you read this, please do not forget to educate your people that the corruption is not alone in Africa but also coming from your own leaders of the so-called free world.

The Western government is responsible for the

majority of assassinations and coup plotting in Africa and against the African people. While remaining under the cloak of darkness they are executing our great leaders to fulfil their own selfish interests.

IF IT WAS NOT FOR AFRICA

James Baldwin: *"Now, we are speaking about expense; I suppose there are several ways to address oneself, too, some attempt to define what that word means here. Let me put it this way; from a very little point of view, the harbours and the ports and the railroads of the country, the economy, especially of the Southern state, could not conceivably be what it has become if they had not had and do not still have indeed for so long, for many generations, cheap labour. I am stating very seriously; this is not an overstatement that I picked the cotton and I carried it to market, and I built the railroad under someone else's whip for nothing, for nothing. The Southern oligarchy, which has until today so much power in Washington and therefore some power in the world, was created by my labour and my sweat, and the violation of my women and the murder of my children. This, in the land of the free and the home of the brave, and no one can challenge that statement: it is a matter of historical record. And in another way, this dream – I will get to the dream in a moment – is at the expense of the American Negro."*

This is a little piece to remind the world of some of the gifts that Africa and her people have given to the world. This is for those who think that Africans are the problem, so why not hate and discriminate?

If it was not for Africa, America would have never had legends like: Muhammad Ali, Michael Jordan, Ray Charles, Michael Johnson, Allyson Felix, Daniel Hale William, Althea Gibson, Whitney Houston, Serena and Venus Williams, Arthur Ash, Tiger Woods, Jesse Owen, Barry Sounders, Ray Lewis, John Randle, Chad Johnson, Barry Bonds, Wilma Rudolph, Simone Biles, Florence Griffith-Joyner, Dave Chappelle, Kevin Hart, Eddie Murphy, James brown, Denzel Washington, Michael Jackson and the Jackson five, Aretha Franklin, Barry White, Marvin Gay, Malcolm X, Barack Obama and Michelle Obama, Tupac Shakur, George Forman, Garret Morgan, Mike Tyson, Carl Lewis and Morgan Freeman.

If it was not for Africa, Dorothy Vaughan, Mary Jackson and Katherine Goble Johnson, NASA would have never won the space race, to name a few. If it was not for Africa, the US would have never been the dominant force in the summer Olympic Games and other world sporting events. If it was not for Africa, the American music culture would have never been the same. If it was not for Africa, the American economy would be like a third world country, and America would not be celebrating its education and innovation in the history books today.

If it was not for Africa, the famous 'I have a dream' speech by Martin Luther King Jr would have never been heard.

If it was not for Africa, France would have never

won the World Cup in 2018; there would have never been the likes of: Gael Monfils, Thierry Henry, Marcel Desailly, Lilian Thuram, Dimitri Bascou, Jo Wilfred Tsonga, Eloyse Lesueur, Emmanuel Biron, Benjamin Campaore, Christine Arron, Eunice Barber and Marc Raquil. If it was not for Africa, France would have never had a French Open Champion in 1983, Yannick Noah, and countless other entertainers, musicians, doctors, politicians and educationists. If it was not for Africa, the French economy would be worse than in a third world country.

If it was not for Africa, Great Britain would have never celebrated amazing champions like: Mo Farah, Nicola Adams, Denise Lewis, Kelly Holmes, Jessica Ennis, Lennox Lewis, Lewis Hamilton, Linford Christie, Tessa Sanderson, Dina Asher-Smith, Kare Adenegan, Maggie Alphonsi, Christine Ohuruogu, Asha Philip, Anne Wafula Strike, Alice Dearing, John Barnes, Rio Ferdinand, Ashley Cole, Emile Heskey, Viv Anderson, Ian Wright, Paul Ince, Sol Campbell and David James. Not forgetting the great doctors, bus, train and taxi drivers, social workers, teachers, musicians and great inventors whose continuous contributions to the economy have made Great Britain a household name in sports, music, entertainment and education in the world. If it was not for Africa, Great Britain would have never been a global economic powerhouse.

If it was not for Africa, Germany would have never celebrated these people: Jerome Boateng, Ivy Quainoo, Roberto Blanco, Alyn Camara, Antonio Rudiger, Dennis Aogo and many more.

If it was not for Africa, Japan would never have had a four-time grand slam tennis champion and former world number one, Naomi Osaka. Africa is to thank for the likes of Abdul Hakim Sani Brown, Rui Hachimura, Louis Okoye, Airi Miyabe, Ariana Miyamoto and many more.

Spain enjoys the likes of Fatima Diame, Vicente Engonga, Ansu Fati and Adama Traore amongst others.

In Belgium and the Netherlands, they have bundled a list of great Africans or African descendants who make amazing athletes who dominate their track, field and other sporting events around the world as well as in educational departments and economic areas too, and their national football team.

We have seen Greek basketball star Giannis Antetokounmpo.

In Italy, we have seen the likes of Mario Balotelli.

In Qatar, high jumper legend Mutaz Essa Barshim.

In China, they have Hui Ding.

Switzerland boasts Mujinga Kambundji, Yvon Mvogo, Francois Moubandji, Breel Embolo, Denis Zakaria and many more.

If it was not for Africa, the island of Jamaica would have never seen the likes of Usain Bolt, who brings the world and people together through his charismatic attitude, love and passion for running. We would have never seen Shelly-Ann Fraser, Asafa Powell, Veronica Campbell Brown, Yohan Blake, Bob Marley, Mark Anthony Myrie (Buju Banton) and the first Jamaican bobsled team made up of Devon Harris, Dudley Stokes, Michael White, Freddy Powell and Chris Stokes in Calgary, Alberta, Canada in 1988. I can say the same thing for all the other islands and Caribbean countries such as the Bahamas, Barbados, Dominican Republic, Guyana, Cayman Islands, Trinidad and Tobago, Suriname, Grenada, Saint Lucia etc.

In Brazil, Africa gave us Pele and the endless list of great athletes that the nation has produced worldwide.

If it was not for Africa, the English Premier League would have never seen the likes of Didier Drogba, Mo Salah, Sadio Mane, Emmanuel Adebayo, Jay-Jay Okocha, Nwankwo Kanu, Yaya Toure, Michael Essien and the list goes on.

If it was not for Africa, traffic lights would not exist as it was Garrett Morgan who invented them. The first open-heart surgery would not have taken place if it were not for Dr Daniel Hale Williams. If it was not for Africa, the hundreds of thousands to millions of men who were brought to Europe to fight for their colonial masters in the First and Second World Wars would have never existed. If it was not for Africa, the world super powers' economies and standards of living today would have never risen to such heights.

Africa has given the world a thousand times more than what the world has thanked, appreciated, and praised Africa for. It amazes me how in 2020, we Africans and black people are fighting for equal rights with campaigns such as Black Lives Matter, even though we have given everyone more than they could have asked for! The super world powers could change all this in a year, but because of superiority, greed and selfish ambitions, they will do everything in their power to never change anything for Africa and her people.

This is why I believe that it is our duty as Africans to learn our own history and make these changes. We must stand against any influence that will corrupt, impoverish, and dehumanise our culture, freedom and dignity. The development and progress of Africa is solely in our hands.

Land is the only property that will give someone power and status, so we should not be selling any piece to anyone who is not African. Africans do not own any massive land area outside Africa, but many nations from around the world now owns half of our land. We must change that and take full control of our continent because the one who controls the land has the power, wealth and the ability to make decisions.

The prediction is that in the next ten to fifteen years, Africa could have one of the best economies in the world.

That is only if we, Africans, and our leaders make this our number one priority.

IF IT WAS LEFT TO AFRICA

All around the world, children are taught from a young age about the contributions that the Western world have made to Africa. This makes it seem like Africa cannot live without foreign aid or outside help and suggests that Africa has not contributed much to the world. This is not the case because Africans have been living healthily and peacefully for thousands of years before any other civilisation. Historic fabrications and misleading stories have led those people from around the world to believe that they are better than others (especially Africans). This is not because they were born racist or born superior to others but because they have been led to think that way deliberately.

This is the cause of 21st century racial hatred and discrimination. I am part of this wonderful human race, but I continue to experience racism first-hand. We are labelled as the most dangerous people on the surface of the Earth. In the world of Africa, we know this is not true, so I wrote my checklist for people to use to help them truly understand Africa, and to realise they have been taught wrong by their educators and historians.

- If it was left to Africans, there would never have been guns.
- The First and Second World Wars would not have

taken place.

- The atomic bomb would have never been dropped on the Japanese people in Hiroshima.
- Napalm bombs would have never killed millions of Vietnamese.
- The Iraqis would have never faced the war and devastation that they went through and lost tens of thousands of their people.
- If it had been left to us African people, AIDS, Ebola and many other diseases would have never existed on this planet.
- If it had been left to us, racism would not exist on this Earth, and everyone would be treated equally with respect and humility.
- If it was left to us, the people of Afghanistan, Libya, Palestine, Israel and Lebanon would have never experienced modern day weapons, war, political, religious and social injustice.
- If it had been left to us, Africa would never have heard of Apartheid. We would never have had to fight among ourselves over religion; we would never have experienced racism at scale.
- If it was left to us, 120 million people would not have lost their lives through trans-Atlantic

slavery.

- If it was left to us, no race would have suffered over 400 years of hate, injustice and brutality through slavery, colonisation and imperialism rules and laws to exploit others forcefully.
- If it was left to us, inequality, social injustice, bullets and brutality would never have existed.
- If it was left to us, no other race would be screaming "I cannot breathe" as they died while we or our government stood there and did nothing.

When Africans are viewed as primitive, corrupt, criminals and thieves, I laugh inside in disbelief, because there are records to show that we have caused only 1% of all the damage and atrocities being permanently committed against us locally and globally.

We are feared around the world, not because we are bad or dangerous but because we have been systematically and deliberately misrepresented through propaganda on every level of media and educational platforms. Governments and supremacists around the world have done this for centuries because they want to be the superior races. If anything, we have given life to mankind and have built the global economy through slavery, our natural resources, and innovation. Yet all we get is hate, injustice and the most brutal, inhumane treatment in the history of mankind because of our skin colour, our strength, natural wealth, culture and empathy for others. This is 2022, and we are tired of being humiliated around the world. It is about time for humanity to come together as one family because without us, no one would be here today. We should have the same rights and freedom to live on Earth too.

QUESTIONS

I travel a lot and I often see other cultures and how they are progressing or how they are being challenged. When I see how our people are portrayed on TV, especially in the US, I ask myself questions about the Africa I know. When people ask me about the horrors of Africa, I question the African continent and our leaders even more. In the end, I find that there are endless questions to be answered by Africans, for our people and our future. Below are some questions that go through my mind; please feel free to answer them and see what you can do to make changes and help make Africa a better place for all.

- Do we even want to be a superpower? If so, what can we do to make Africa a superpower?
- What are the lessons we have learnt from our past?
- How are we going to defend and protect Africa if the continent is attacked?
- Why is our education system so poor? Who is to blame for that?
- Why can we not have one African currency?
- Why can we not have one passport?

- Why can we not produce the finished products from our raw materials?
- Why can we not have the best universities?
- Why all the wars?
- Why are children who live on the street not being taken into consideration?
- Why do the US, France and other countries have military bases in Africa?
- How come Africa has not got any powerful military bases in the Western world?
- Why, with everything that we have, is Africa still dependent on aid?
- Why is China buying land in Africa and not the other way around?
- Why do we produce raw materials that are turning into trillions of dollars, but we Africans make only a fraction of that?
- Why can we not unite?
- Why do we still let the outside world dictate to us?
- Why does Africa never take a strong stance against brutality to our people around the world?
- Why are we so disrespected around the world?

- Why are so many Africans trying to run away from Africa?
- Why are our people dying in the Mediterranean Sea just to come to Europe?
- Why do our leaders put their money in Western banks?
- Why do our leaders only go for medical checks and treatments in the Western world or China?
- Is Africa's health system good for the people?
- Why are we not producing our own pharmaceuticals?
- Why are we not producing our own brands of cars, planes, mobile phones, computers, trains and all the other technological products when we have all the raw materials?
- Why can we as Africans not be self-sufficient enough to have a good standard of living?
- Why has Africa's economy been so bad for the past 100 years?
- Why have we been praying for the past 60 years and are still waiting for God when nothing has changed?
- Why do we let others interfere with our business?

- Why do we not write our history books and produce our own movies portraying our true heritage and teach it to the world?
- Why are we, the 1.3 billion people in Africa, afraid of those who are dragging Africa to her knees?
- What do the 54 nations' leaders want for their people?
- Why are none of the European and Western countries being held responsible for the damage done to Africa and her people?
- Who is allowing all the guns that are used to slaughter our people to come to Africa?
- Who is paying for the guns and why?
- Where are they getting the money from for all the weapons and wars in Africa?
- Why is the price of our resources never set by Africans?
- Why is the African Union so weak?
- Why is Africa in debt with all her wealth of natural resources?
- Why have we not got a universal language based on one of our 3000 plus African languages?

- How come we have the richest continent but have the poorest nations?
- Why is all the waste from around the world being dumped in Africa?
- When are Africans going to wake up and begin to take the right and necessary action?
- Why do others have to come and help us with water when we have some of the biggest, longest and deepest rivers?
- How come there is starvation in Africa to the point that others have to come to our aid?
- Why can we as Africans not manage and take care of ourselves?
- Are we not capable of building a great educational system and sustainable economy?
- Are we not capable of building great technology in Africa?
- What is the real amount of wealth stolen from Africa each year?
- What have we done to deserve all the humiliation from around the world?
- Will Africa ever get reparation from her colonial states?

- Maybe you have your own questions…

Until we find answers, it will be harder for us to find a way to progress. Africa needs to wake up, stand up and keep moving forward for her people.

AFRICA'S FUTURE AND WAY FORWARD

If you have read this far you may be thinking that Sam spends a lot of time looking at the dark side of Africa! I can tell you that the future of Africa is looking brighter as the years go by thanks to today's technology. Many younger people in the continent are able to see what the rest of the world is like without stepping foot outside of Africa. The fact that many Africans are now willing to return home and help with its development is a great start for us, but we still have a long way to go.

My only problem with the way our young people act is that they want to be Westernised because of what they have seen on TV or the internet. Well, there is nothing wrong with that but they must embrace progress while preserving their own African culture. It is one of our greatest assets, if we lose that, then we will continue to lose our sense of origin which is the key to who we are.

When we talk about Africa's future, we must not forget that this will only be possible through a united Africa. This means our own common language, currency, central bank, passport, education system, and traveling privileges throughout Africa. We also need free education for all, good medical and health care systems for the entire continent, and great leaders and transparent governance that will inspire and create a better future for the younger generation. A future where we make sure that all our resources are mined, produced, priced and controlled by us, and that all leaders and people with wealth only use an African-created bank.

Wealth must be spread equally among nations, and we must fight to eliminate debt, loans and aid from elsewhere. We are wealthy enough to be able to fix our problems without others dictating to us. We must grow our own food, and not use modernised, processed food or plants created outside Africa. The food we grow should be free from chemicals. We must refuse all unwanted waste from outside of Africa that is polluting and causing harm to our continent and our people.

The Younger Generation

The younger generation have the power to stand up and make changes for a better future for Africa. You must be proud and patriotic to your nation, yet also believe in Africa first. Women must be treated equally, and we must make it part of our collective mission to empower and motivate women and girls so that they can play their part in making Africa a better place. If women are empowered, Africa will become a free, independent and successful continent.

Make sure that you are not led to be influenced by colonial powers and imperialist states. Question everything, even our leaders. They are there to serve the people, the people are not there to serve them.

When you hear of some foreign billionaire bringing novel pharmaceuticals to Africa, ask yourself why they are experimenting on our people and who is allowing them to do so? When you hear that some western fast-food company wants to 'support' a school, what is the real reason? When a soft drinks conglomerate offers to 'support' kids with free sugar and chemical laden drinks, ask why they do not spend the money on safe water for those same kids? Understand that it is rare that any outside country, company or organisation sends its people into Africa for the sole purpose and benefit of Africa's citizens. That is not to say that all those from outside do not have an altruistic intent, but, sadly, we have more than enough experience to see altruism used as a disguise for more vested interests, sometimes with sinister motives.

War and Guns

You must say no to weapons and wars. The only use for guns is to destroy lives, communities and civilisations. It is big business for those that are manufacturing them too; we are losing lives, wealth and our future just by accepting arms into our communities. We must say no. No to guns and no to war. In the Western world, guns are given to trained military and police personnel who are there to safeguard their citizens. In Africa, we have too many young, bright and vibrant people who are

Africa's next generation of leaders, fighting and dying in civil conflicts that are created by some of the colonial states. We are killing our continent by taking up arms and slaughtering our own people, while at the same time those that created and brought the guns to us are stealing our wealth. I urge you to say no to anyone, even if they are from your own family, tribe or community, you must not take up arms and destroy lives. Africa does not need war or guns; we need education and innovation. We have been divided and corrupted over the past hundreds of years, and it is about time we stopped all that and started to build our continent the way we want it to be.

Religions and Tribalism Used to Divide Us

Believe whatever you choose to believe, but that should not make you hate your neighbours or other tribes. It is in all religious books to 'love thy neighbour' and to not kill. So put your religion aside and do not use it as a reason to inflict pain and suffering on others. God will never reward you for destroying the lives of his creation.

Your religious beliefs are your personal connection with your god and should not be used to take the rights and freedoms away from others. You must not hate others because they choose to believe in something different to you. We as Africans must learn to be tolerant of others in our communities and treat them with respect and humility, just like we have done to colonial masters from around the world. We have to care for our people and protect our communities from killings in the name of religion. There is no reward for killing, and there is definitely no heaven for killers.

As the great Bob Marley said in one of his love songs: "There is one question I'd really love to ask; Is there a place for a hopeless sinner who has hurt all mankind just to save his own beliefs? Let's get together and feel alright."

There is no place for such people. So please, my African people – especially the younger generations – this is the time for you all to say no to religious hate and violence. You have the power to make tremendous and positive changes. Even in families we argue because we all have our differences, but we must not fight and destroy each other because of those differences. Our differences are there to be celebrated.

The many tribes and cultures we have in Africa are truly beautiful things that you will not find in any other part of the world. We are unique and blessed with a diversity of wonderful people and cultural depth. We must love and do our best to appreciate all our tribes and cultures. Tribalism can be just another form of hate. If we are crying and complaining that our people were chained, tied up, beaten and lynched during slavery, then why are we doing the very same today by creating a form of tribalism? It is like what happened in Rwanda in 1994, the genocide between the Tutsi and the Hutu, which was influenced by some of our own people as well as outsiders. We do not want these sorts of things to happen in Africa anymore. We must say no to such influences, either internally or externally. When these things happen, all we have done is played into the hands of the supremacists who want to maintain division and negative press around the world. It will surely not build a peaceful and progressive Africa, thus making our young people want to leave and go beyond our shores.

We must look at Africa as a great sailing ship. We must plan the journey ahead and be prepared to navigate ourselves to the destination of our choosing. We must not allow others to create their plan for us and take over the helm that we should be steering. You, the youth, need to take control of it now and come together as one people, no matter what nationality you belong to. We must think as one Africa. If we do not, then we are only serving the colonial powers' interests of exploitation that keeps us fighting each other and destroying our future. Every one of us should refrain from religious hatred and tribalism. These ideologies should have no place in our society, and it is time to let go of them to begin to resolve, together, the challenges that face our continent. After all, no one will do it for us.

Africa's future and the way forward is to think and act as one community. We need education for all, unity, self-innovation, and must not let anyone influence us in any shape or form that will diminish our freedom, peace, humility and justice. A creative and progressive interest is all we need. We have the power to say no to Europe, America, and China. All nations have a right to freedom and to make their own decisions of governance in the interests of the citizens they serve; so do we as Africans. We are free to deal with our continent's problems and we are capable of doing so for our own good. We have endured too much. We must not allow the repetition of the mistakes from the past. We must now take full control of the future of Africa and her people wherever they may be. This is our responsibility as Africans and the future is in the hands of our children.

THE WAY I SEE THE WORLD

The world is our home. The world is our family. The world is our playground. So let us all play like one big family because we have a limited time to live on this Earth. In my experience, I fear nothing but man, because we are capable of inflicting the most ferocious pain on each other with no empathy. I am not worried about going to heaven because I know I am doing God's work, not because I go to any religious house of worship and show everyone that I am godly, but because I treat all mankind with love, care and respect, and I treat everything that is on our Earth with care too. As James Baldwin said, "If you are afraid to die, you may never live, and no one knows anything about death."

Living on this Earth, I now realise what is going wrong with humanity; we have centred our lives and values through monetary systems, wealth, fame, material things and fortunes. Therefore, we have lost our natural ability to love and care for others. We now see others for how much wealth they have accumulated in their lifetime.

The difference between the poor and the rich is shocking, the scale has always been tipped in favour of the financial supremacists because they designed the scales. It is long overdue that they be held accountable for their actions. The scales must be balanced in a way that no one has their interests set above others.

When I look at weddings, I see the difference in wealth. When I look at funerals, I see the difference in wealth and fame. When I look at the roads filled with cars, I see the difference in wealth and fortunes. When I look at cities, towns and homes, I see the difference in wealth. When I look at schools, colleges and universities, I see the difference in wealth. But when I look at humanity in general, the difference we can see is that 99.9% of all wealth is controlled by less than 1% of the people. When the richest people on earth collectively control the banks, the land, the media, and more, then they effectively control us. Time to change that.

This world would be a better place if we chose to pause and look at the beauty of this Earth and humanity, with all the bountiful gifts that God and nature has given us. If we share them among us equally, then we can start to love more, care more, laugh more. We will all live in peace and harmony for our lifetime on Earth. We do not have to wait for heaven to experience that.

The true character of a sincere and pure human being is not about wealth or material things, but the love, care, respect and humility we show to our fellow human beings and all creatures of this world. The people you leave behind will only remember you for your loving and caring heart towards them, and not because of your possessions, fortunes or status.

When I look at graveyards, I can also see the difference

in wealth by how some people's graves are laid and engraved. But the truth of the matter is, your possessions and glories through life will not guarantee you a passage to heaven. So, let us be kind to each other, we are God's people of this world.

THE ILLUSION OF DEMOCRACY

Around the world today there is an illusion that we are living in democratic societies. Many people around the world trust and put their faith in the hands of their government; most of these people are not directly affected by some of the consequences that others go through on a daily basis. In my opinion, there is no such thing as democracy for all. It does not exist and will never do so. Not as long as the wealth of this world is controlled by less than 1% of the world population, and only a handful of nations are allowed to invade other countries and terrorise them under the guise of democracy and the fraud of global peace. So long as these are the same nations with the power to hold the so-called nuclear deterrent, then there will be no such thing as democracy.

In the reality of our existence today, the whole world is living under a communist state in the name of democracy. Do you ever wonder why there are approaching eight billion people on Earth but only 1% have the power? Do you wonder why Africa, with nearly 1.4 billion people, the wealthiest continent by natural resources, has not got the power to control the world like the West does?

Do you ever wonder why people are afraid to speak the truth? Why are you not allowed to say this or that? Well, this is because those 1% of people have the army, police, and the law on their side to oppress you if you do not behave by the rules they set. You and I know that if you step out of line, they will come after you with no mercy.

In this light, we cannot be claiming that we are free and living in a democratic society if we are afraid of speaking and standing up for the truth. Democracy should not cause fear in people; quite the opposite, this is what you expect in a communist state. Democracy is an illusion to benefit those 1% of people, and they do not care about the 99% of humanity so long as they are in control.

A MESSAGE TO ALL MANKIND

As I come to conclude this book and will one day reach the end of my journey on this Earth, I am hoping that as an old man I will be able to watch the younger African generations, dancing, singing, and looking forward to their future. I would like to believe that I have played my part in inspiring them. I would like to smile knowing that I have created a path for many. I would like to be in heaven knowing that my children and grandchildren will not go through hate, injustice, discrimination, and suffering as my generation and those before me did.

At the end of the day, we are all human beings living under one sky. You may be white, black, brown or whatever your colour is, because that is the beauty of God and nature's creation. We did not choose the colour of our skin; we did not choose to be born rich or poor. We did not choose to be born in Africa, or Europe, or the Americas; it is in our rite of passage to be who we are. To hate someone for where they come from, or the colour of their skin, or their religion, gender, and beliefs, serves nothing but to deny another human being of their freedom, justice and equality as a rightful citizen of this Earth.

You may have more privilege than others. You may live in a mansion. You may drive the best car, eat in the best restaurants, have the best education, live in a developed country, and wear the most expensive clothes in the world, but at the end of the day, your status does not define who you are; the way you treat others does. LOVE is the fuel to care for others, EMPATHY is the heart that allows us to seek kindness, and APPRECIATION for other people is the only peaceful solution to live side by side with one another and share our common beautiful cultures, languages, races, religions, and our greatest gift of all: LIFE.

We have already seen how wars have brought further hate and loss of lives; that life is a precious gift, and we must nurture and cherish it. We have enough to deal with as people, and this is why I am urging you to refrain from supporting any government, company or individual whose ambition is to divide the bond and spirit of humanity to satisfy their own greed, You may feel remote from that destruction, but the way the supremacists are steering us as I write this, people of the world have never seen such a threat that will affect everyone. You may not be in the shoes of a victim of a war in Africa, you may feel comfortable enough where you are now, but I assure you, everyone will be touched by what is coming unless we all act now, as one, to prevent it.

As humans, we are not created to be enemies, we are not born to hate or discriminate against others; this is something our societies have taught us. You must always show compassion for your fellow human beings no matter who or what they are.

We must strive to reduce some of the human activities that we participate in for economic gain that cause so much destruction to our planet. By looking at some of the natural and unnatural global disasters over the past decades, one can see that we are only turning our planet into a time bomb. I believe we must act now before it is too late.

We must also protect our children from abuse and torture. We should give them meaningful and unbiased education, and teach them to care, love and have empathy for others. We have to set the example and be good role models. We must be kind and leave them a better and more peaceful world far away from the fear of future disaster.

When someone asked me to be kind, I replied, "No need to tell me to be kind because I have been kind since the day I began to walk on this Earth. You look at yourself and show me how kind you are, and how firm you stand against discrimination, hate and injustice for others?" For me as an African and a citizen of this Earth, I see it as my duty to always be kind to everyone, including those who have caused me pain and trauma. I know sometimes my kindness has got me into all sorts of trouble, but I continue to choose kindness because if I do not, I may hurt innocent people. If you are concerned about kindness, please look at yourself and tell your people to be kind to others, because I have always been kind to you and everyone I come across. It must not be something you turn on and off, it must be a habit for life, a purpose for which you are known by others. Imagine if you can influence one other person to pay forward a positive action? That would be 365 people influenced in a year. What if they did the same thing? Now that would be a pandemic we would welcome.

We are not enemies today. Certain situations, conditions, and circumstances may have been created to form an illusion that we are enemies. Those pulling the strings can profit in every direction from what they have started. They can supply weapons to both sides, they can create a media deluge that pits us against each other. At a point of their choosing, usually as the money for arms run out, they will step forward as peacekeepers to provide the solution to our warring problem. Let us love more, respect more, smile and laugh more so that we can live in peace with our natural differences without the need to hate or discriminate because someone is different. Most of all, let us live like one big human citizenship with equal rights, freedom, and justice for all.

Thank you for giving me your time. I hope what I have said, albeit brief, has given you a perspective of our continent. I hope it will help you be part of the solution for an amazingly wonderful future, so that Africa can leave behind, but never forget, its tragic history. No-one can break the African spirit.

Sam P Jalloh

Lightning Source UK Ltd.
Milton Keynes UK
UKHW011144240123
415874UK00004B/128

9 781914 560491